BETTER WRITING

Better Writing

BY

HENRY SEIDEL CANBY, PH.D.

EDITOR OF "THE SATURDAY REVIEW OF LITERATURE";
DEPARTMENT OF ENGLISH, YALE UNIVERSITY

New York
HARCOURT, BRACE AND COMPANY

26·10353

PRINTED IN THE U S. A BY
QUINN & BODEN COMPANY, INC,
RAHWAY, N. J.

CONTENTS

BETTER WRITING

CHAPTER I

INTRODUCTION

THE art of writing, like every other art, is simpler in practice than the books about it. Good writing is perhaps as difficult as good playing on the piano, more difficult than good cooking, less difficult than good living, but to know *how* to do it is no great secret. As Dogberry said, with more wisdom than was intended, "to be a well-favoured man is the gift of fortune, but to write and read comes by nature." It is natural to write well, if you think well; the mechanical details of mere writing have been taught to any one past middle childhood a hundred times—which unfortunately does not mean that he has learned them once.

I say mere writing because there is a belief abroad that sets of rules and special courses can make short-story writers and playwrights, or guarantee the composition of business letters or reports that will win immediate success. This is, of course, superstition. Rhetoric cannot make brain power or English Composition teach the complexities of life and the drama thereof. The power to think and the ability to arouse and control emotion are products of heredity plus the whole of education, including every useful experience

3

in life, and this power and this ability lie behind all writing and condition its excellence. Yet in every profession or business that requires the use of words there is a process like the passage of a nervous thrill from the brain to the body in which whatever is to be said or written has to be composed and translated into language. Whether one writes a chapter or a letter, a play or an advertisement, that movement and that process exist. The fertile mind of H. G. Wells and the less active intellect of the bond salesman about to construct a letter, must at some time discharge their very different cargoes by the same machinery of mere writing. Mr. Wells requires a much more complicated process, but the principles, so far as they are used in common, are the same.

This is a book, not on poetry or story-telling or play-writing or letter-writing, but on writing, the neck of the bottle through which they all have to go. It is not a book on sentences, paragraphs, and the rest of the mechanics of writing, nor is it designed for students who still need drill in the elements of composition. Such books exist by millions of copies and every one has studied them and can do so again if he wishes. They teach how the engine works; this book deals with the relation between the machine and the driver, with the relation between ideas and the expression thereof. Or, to put it differently, what follows is for the student who has just completed an English composition course in school or college, or for the older writer who has studied how English ought to be put together, who knows in theory what ought to be done, and yet still feels muscle-bound when he wants to write.

There are no grades in this experience. The editor encounters the same disabilities in mere writing that the teacher wrestles with in a university. Age brings experience worth writing about, but not necessarily the means of writing it. Many a specialist (especially in America) understands his subject from the protoplasm up and yet cannot write well about it; many a wise woman understands human nature to its inmost core, and yet cannot write a story. The research paper of a great scholar, the first novel of a man of thirty, the story written for a college magazine, the essay of a sophomore, may differ a thousand-weight in the nature of their contents, and yet be fit to go on the same shelf as exhibits of failure in mere writing. Writers may differ in years from the usual age of those who study textbooks to sixty (when William De Morgan began to write fiction), and in their capacity as human beings from a saturation of worldly experience to that dilute solution which here in America we call being educated, and yet need a new conception of what makes good writing.

James Joyce, the Irish novelist, in his much discussed book *Ulysses,* has taken many hundred pages to tell the story of twenty-four hours in the life of a group of Dublin acquaintances, and Virginia Woolf in her *Mrs. Dalloway* has made a novel from an even briefer period. But what is said, and what happens, in these books is conditioned by all the past of the characters and by all their hopes for the future. There is a fair analogy here with writing—every kind of writing. After reflection, emotion, study, inspiration, command, after any experience which makes writing necessary, comes the moment of composition. That moment is the heart of writing—of all writing. And when the ideas are grasped and composed and begin to be set down in English, the heart begins to beat and writing passes from thought into practice. The purpose of this book is to describe what must happen in a writer's mind if, with something worth writing about, he is to write not badly but well.

When an idea gets hold of you, you must go.

Chapter II

IDEAS

IDEAS are the most valuable commodities in the world, and good ideas, unfortunately, the rarest. Books on writing often assume that we go about jingling like the Red Knight in *Through the Looking Glass* with ideas strung to our saddle bows waiting to be used. Or their authors realize in a panic that their victims must have something to write about, and so present the unfortunate student with fifty assorted ideas for experiment. No wonder the results are so unsatisfactory, for live writing will no more grow from dead ideas (or indeed from any ideas not personal to the writer) than a live fish from a dead cell.

It is possible to talk for an hour with never an idea, and some lecturers accomplish the feat, and it is possible to write English for pages with never a clear idea, which is the reason for much bad writing. But behind good talk and behind good writing ideas stand dominant. It is impossible to discuss good writing without first describing the function of an idea.

I am using "idea" in its loose colloquial sense which covers both a perception and a thought. In practice,

7

one builds into the other and the two together govern expression. Of ideas in this general sense there are two kinds, the expected and the unexpected. With the unexpected idea only creative writers of talent need concern themselves. A sudden resemblance flashes out of the blue and gives the theme of a story, the situation for a play, the point of an essay, the gist of a speech. Some Babbitt in a smoking-car reveals himself to a Sinclair Lewis as the key to What Is Wrong with America; Matthew Arnold discovers in a lucid moment that the whole of his philosophy is to see life steadily and to see it whole; Huck Finn realizes that there is something wrong with a morality that tells him to uphold slavery and yet love the runaway slave. It is usually impossible to make such ideas come at will, although the house may be swept, garnished, and made ready for them. A fortunate impact of external stimulus upon an open mind is required, and indeed many excellent writers have described the moment at which ideas came as one of subdued excitement when suddenly and without evident reason the idea was born. Thinking hard never brings an idea with any certainty, but ideas never come except after brooding, reflection, and thought in a brain that has worked with full power. Get your mind whirling, says William James, and see what happens. Emerson jotted down his flashes in his journal and made essays of them afterward. Dickens and Hawthorne did the same with the plots and situations which came to them. Much modern poetry of the impressionistic kind is nothing but rhythmic notes of ideas caught on the wing.

There is a beautiful example of the birth of an unexpected idea (scientific in this case, not literary) in Sinclair Lewis's *Arrowsmith,* where on pages 257 ff. and 308 ff. the author describes the discovery of "phage." I quote only a relevant passage. The idea— what the discovery might mean—is implied rather than stated, and properly, since the scientist should emphasize his experiment rather than any preconceived theory. But the flash of discovery and then the painful working out are quite as in literature:

He was playing with cultures isolated from various dairies and various people, thinking mostly of Klopchuk and streptococcus. Accidentally he discovered the lavish production of hemolysin in sheep's blood as compared with the blood of other animals. Why should streptococcus dissolve the red blood corpuscles of sheep more easily than those of rabbits? . . . He sat for hours meditating.

There is another in Lincoln's Gettysburg address, where the brief speech is built backward, so to speak, from the famous idea, perfectly phrased, which concludes it—"that government of the people, by the people, for the people, shall not perish from the earth"; and a monumental example in Darwin's *Origin of Species,* since that epoch-making book is an attempt to verify a simple modification of an old idea, namely, that evolution, which the Greeks conceived of, might proceed by natural selection.

In a book merely on writing, like this one, only simple advice can be given as regards unexpected ideas; namely, that you should be ready for them and fasten them to the memory when they appear. Many a good story, and many an excellent poem, has never been written because the idea slipped from the mind and was lost. To go further would be to discuss the springs of genius and the processes of creative mind, which is far beyond the scope of this eminently practical treatise.

All this is, or should be, familiar, yet curious delusions appear. That lack of self-confidence which psychologists call our inferiority complex and which stalls so many honest writers halfway along the road of their thoughts, is often due to the absurd notion that one must wait for some unexpected inspiration before writing can proceed. Most of the writing that needs to be done has no concern whatever with creative ideas that are original in character and novel in effect, but is a useful, if uninspired, working out of what the writer knows and the reader does not. Let the genius and the creative spirit fade out of the picture and consider instead the plain bread and butter of writing. It is not so very plain after all, for there are a thousand varieties, of which the simplest is, given so many facts, or so much circumstance, or such and such a plot, how to handle them effectively, how to get the material from your mind to another's. The idea is expected, not unexpected; it is there waiting in sight, and you go after it. There is no mystery in the process, but as much difficulty as genius may experience.

This is the text and theme of all rhetoric books, and the things that one is told to do or not to do in such practical writing are multitudinous; yet almost invariably the essential beginning of the process is left out. You know this or that; you are told that, to write this or that, such and such methods are available. That is all. The idea behind, which if expected and easily formed is nevertheless precisely as much a living cell, personally created and personally felt as the more original conception of a genius, is passed over as of little importance. It is the machinery of writing, not writing itself, which is discussed.

"The writer," says the textbook, "wishes to explain how radio operates (or how to find birds' nests, or how to write an editorial on the League of Nations, or how to describe the idea of God). He must make a plan, and this holds true whether he is proposing to explain or to tell a story. He must proceed from the known to the unknown, or he must divide his subject into sections which do not overlap, or he must proceed from cause to effect, or from effect to cause."

Not so fast. This arbitrary chopping up and reassorting of knowledge for general consumption is what makes so much dull, unintelligent writing, and so many dull writers who think of writing as an intolerable nuisance. The victim of this method never wished to write of radios, or birds' nests, or the League of Nations, or the idea of God. He could not conceivably want, or need, to write about anything with which his mind was not already well stocked. And granted a ripe subject, the first importance attaches not to a plan or a method but to the idea which he forms of it in his own mind.

Here are the facts of the case—what needs to be said of them? Here are the circumstances—what is the plot of the story? The idea must crystallize before writing begins. The clearest relationships must be established within the material before any plan is made; otherwise the writing is bound to be dull, even if it is as clear as it is insignificant. Toss, in a conversation, a new theme to the "know-it-all" variety of talker, and you can hear him for five minutes elaborate, discuss, dissect, with never a faulty sentence and never an incoherent thought, and yet substantially say nothing, mean nothing. You have remarked that Great Britain in her political problems is twenty years ahead of the United States and he, missing the idea of contrast and difference which is the root of the matter, will discourse of socialism with lucidity, emphasis, and wordy irrelevance.

There are curious examples of this familiar to the

practiced reader—and by no means all of them are
to be found in schoolboy "themes" and deficient
"exercises." Many a short story cracks through its
thin ice of reality because the writer never lucidly
saw at the beginning how his plot and his characters
might move on together. Many an article begins well
and ends in a mass of words because only part of that
idea which should have informed the whole crystallized in the writer's mind.

And while there is every excuse for the writer not
a genius who fails to capture a great and unexpected
idea when he wants one, there is none at all for the
everyday dictator of letters or maker of news stories
who is possessed of his materials and yet fails to get
a clear idea as to what it all means to him and what
he wishes it to mean to others, before he begins to
write.

The question here is not the best way to write—
that comes later. It is an earlier step—a mental self-
searching and appraisal, a process which even in a
business letter is as much emotional as intellectual,
since it means feeling the strength of your subject,
and getting a clear idea as to what that feeling sig-
nifies. There will be more to say later of the results,
and how they may be made to guarantee good writing. What I wish to emphasize here is the importance
of having an idea so clear, so simple, so cogent that
one can put it in a sentence if need be, and yet so
much an idea and so little a rigid plan that only the

thinking out will show what it may mean when developed in full.

There should be an intelligence test through which all ideas, little and big, simple and subtle, would have to pass before writers are allowed to write. "What have you got?" would be the question and the answers would be in sentences, and should infallibly indicate to the critical intelligence whether the labor of writing was likely to be worth while. The tongue-tied author, who has a real idea in his mind but can't express it, would be delayed but not stopped. His idea is caught by only one wing; if he begins to write too soon he will muddle everything. Three versions of a difficult letter, the first inexpressive, the second misleading, the third adequate—and who has not written three such letters—illustrate better than a dozen rules how essential it is to grasp and test the idea first.

Thus ideas must be grasped, molded, developed, whether they are expected and sought for or unexpected gifts from the subconsciousness. Both kinds, when you have them, are relationships between this and that, precisely as a Diesel engine and an old-fashioned pump are both means of converting energy. The value of inspiration and plain everyday finding out what you think of comparatively simple matters awaiting explanation, may be worlds apart, but both— the idea for a tragedy and the idea for a business letter—must be seen and felt in simplicity and clarity before they pass into words. It is like radio. You must tune in, get your wave lengths right, till the thing comes clear and true. A dull mind with a clear idea is better than a facile brain with a muddled thought in it.

CHAPTER III

GRASPING THE IDEA

INTEREST

THE advice, so far, too much resembles the easy order, "Be good, dear child," as if the will to be good and virtue were identical. How does one "tune in" with a subject till the idea comes clear? How create the fortunate ether upon which thought is born, for an idea does not function in waveless space? The answer lies in the magnetic turn of our minds which we call interest, and is explained by the nature of an idea itself.

For an idea is felt before it is thought, as psychologists can demonstrate, and that is the reason why the moment of composition is so important in writing. It is the rise of emotion at a word from another, a sentence in a book, a contradiction, a flashing mountain view, which determines the course of thinking and the subjects of thought. What interests you in the complex of experience always drifting through your mind like cloud racks is what you finally get, what you feel, what makes subjects for your thought. Interest may be exciting and pleasurable, or painful and laborious, but if it is not present you get dead ideas, not live ones.

If you are not interested in your own ideas, it is impossible to feel them with sufficient intensity to start the process of thinking. Indeed, one may go further, and say that the lucid, powerful idea described in the last section is never formed at all unless interest draws it forth and shapes it. Interest is the nurse of ideas. There is, in truth, as much difference between interested and uninterested as between good and bad writing. Not quite the same difference, for it is possible to write clearly and simply of a matter which has no warmth of interest whatever for the writer, but the energy expended in whipping dull dead facts into shape is out of all proportion to the result, which may be passable but never excellent. Interest, if it can be aroused, selects the easy road. Therefore the first great principle in writing is to make your idea interesting to you, or, if the subject springs from some warmth of interest, as is usually the case, to keep that interest warm.

A set of novels by Cooper, Dumas, Scott, Trollope, or Hawthorne illustrates beautifully the functioning of interest. You can run your fingers along the volumes and touch the books where the novelist's mind never kindled to his idea—Hawthorne in *Fanshawe,* Scott in *Count Robert of Paris,* Thackeray in *The Adventure of Philip,* Trollope in one book out of every three.

And there is an excellent example of cooling interest in Rebecca West's novel, *The Judge*. The first half of the book is magnificent; but when the Scotch girl, who is its radiant point, encounters the English mother-in-law who was to be the second node of the story, the writer's interest crosses, diffuses, wavers from one to the other; the idea of the book is more loosely held, the writing grows less brilliant, and the narrative descends toward confusion and almost melodrama. There is an even more striking instance of the reverse in *Romeo and Juliet*. The stale material, probably from an earlier play, which makes up the first act did not warm in Shakespeare's mind. Suddenly, as Juliet appears, his imagination catches fire and the temperature of the play goes up and up until its end. Most fortunate is such writing as Willa Cather's *A Lost Lady*, or the gorgeous odes of John Keats, where an almost passionate warmth of interest embraces the idea from its inception to the last line of the written words. It is not necessary to be passionate in order to write well, but that warmth of mind which we call interest is the soil from which good writing grows, and it alone can make an idea grow sharp and active in the mind.

WHAT HAVE YOU?

If interest alone were enough, all enthusiasts would be good writers and the cool and logical mind would be at a disadvantage. But the interested mind is an asset in writing only in so far as it is a mind as well as interested. This, of course, is a platitude, and to it may be added another, first phrased in this connection by Lucretius, who remarks sagely that nothing comes from nothing. Interest in itself is nothing upon which to write. There must be a noun as well as a qualifying adjective in the proposition, and before discussing the work of the mind in developing an idea, the substance of an idea itself must be further considered.

The truth is that ideas, even unexpected ideas, are crystallizations of what we have already in our consciousness or subconsciousness, crystallizations, in brief, of earlier thought and experience around a fresh nucleus. Beyond what we already have neither interest nor anything else can carry us. It is true that, especially in unexpected ideas, some stimulus from without, some flash of recognition, may change opinion or set knowledge in a new order. Yet the fact remains that nothing comes from nothing, and how the mind is already furnished determines, when it comes to writing, the result.

Viewed this way, the first act of interested writing is to find what you have—which means no more than finding what you know and how you feel about it. An illuminating instance, striking because it is so artificial, is the brief of an argument prepared for debate. A good brief searches and analyzes the contents of

the mind for everything relevant to the proposition
which is to be argued. Why is debating from briefs,
then, usually so dull? Because, in formal debate,
especially the variety usually described in textbooks,
the arguments are merely analyses of what can be
said for or against a topic. There is no warmly held
idea, no interested thinking, behind the brief. But a
really devastating argument, like the pleas for Christian ethics in the New Testament, or Lincoln's
speeches in favor of union, begins with vivid though
simple ideas and sweeps the field to discover evidence.
The genesis of such an argument comes from self-
search, and the result is to draw out the knowledge
and experience which convinced you and will convince
others.

There is a simple and illuminating test of the
process by which an idea clothes itself in the apparel
of your own mind and depends upon the richness of
your thinking for its success. Follow the august
precedents of Chaucer, Shakespeare, Milton, and take
an old plot idea—the Cinderella story, or the fox and
the sour grapes—which, as you first see it, may mean
nothing to you. Then remake it in terms and circumstances of your own experience, warming your interest
as you go—a Hamlet in Wall Street, Lear in the Berkshire Hills.[1] It is done every day, especially upon
the stage, and usually without full consciousness of

[1] Turgenev has done substantially this in his "Lear of the
Steppes."

where the old plot idea came from; and always the working out of the new story is a discovery of what the writer knows of his own people, his own age, his own mind, along lines parallel with the ancient story.

SUBSTANCE

If there can be no good ideas without stuff to make and feed them, the first business of a writer is to get substance for his craft. And certainly what makes so much professional teaching of writing, especially short-story and play writing, ineffective and worse, is the practice of teaching a particular method before the patient has anything to write about, or so much as guesses that he cannot write well until he has something to say. New York is crowded with ineffectual writers searching vainly for bits of experience that will fit in their ready-made play or story formulas. They began with a formula, not with the raw materials of the art of expression.

Why do the Voltaires, the Shaws, the Twains sparkle with ideas while plain John Jenkins surveys blankness in his intellect? There is no answer except that the rain of ideas will patter in one mind and leave another dry for no reason except heredity or good luck. You either have brilliant ideas or you do not have them. But suppose that you have ideas, good, bad, indifferent. What can be done to make them valuable in view of the patent fact that water will not run above its source and no idea can develop in a given brain beyond the resources of that brain? How is the mind of a writer to be stocked for its work? (The resources of a writer's brain are his knowledge of facts, the results of his observations, the richness of his emotions, the vigor of his imagination, the mental training which enables him to see effect in cause and cause in effect.) A well-stored, well-trained brain makes better writing, other things being equal, than a poorly furnished intellect. Of course, the mind can be lumbered with facts, like the hero in Stevenson's *The Wrong Box,* with no result except to trip over them when you try to express yourself. And every one knows that exciting experience does not make a writer: if it did, sailors, policemen, soldiers, and criminal lawyers would be our best authors, and the gentry who write the tales of the Northwest Mounted Police would go to the Barren Lands before instead of after writing about them. Nevertheless, no writer ever had too much assimilated experience, and no writer ever had too much digested education. One-half the trouble (where there is trouble) with American writing today is that the writers cannot write well enough, and the other half is that they do not know enough. For writing is like conversation. The best talk can be supported only by a wide knowledge. No matter how brilliant, a man becomes verbose when he talks beyond his experience. A good idea will break down halfway through a novel because the author simply does not know life well enough to carry on. A sound idea will collapse in the middle of an article because the writer has got beyond his information or fails to grasp the significance of the facts he has gathered.

The first preparation for writing, therefore, is the right kind of education, as much as you can get of it. Nor is it certain that the especial variety of education makes much difference, provided that it sinks in deep and really stirs the mind. The only special education particularly necessary for writers is enough study of language to give a sense of words and enough reading of good literature to get an ear for good expression, a sense of form, and a conception of what writing can do. Beyond this all is grist that comes to the writer's mill, although it must be admitted that what is still called a liberal education, the purpose of which is to prepare for living rather than earning a living, is most relevant to the writer's trade. Science, literature, philosophy, language, and art, studied for the better understanding of man and his universe, are more likely to equip a writer than is a course in mining engineering or applied chemistry. "More likely"— that is all we can say.

For the most of a writer's education will come, of course, from living, from the kind of living which touches the imagination. It is unfortunately true that personal experience, unsought and often tragic, has supplied the material of much good writing. The good writer has usually lived adventurously, which means that he has not been afraid to encounter experience, although the valuable elements of that experience have usually come in his personal relationships rather than on ship decks or battlefields. It used to infuriate Conrad to be told that he was a great writer of the sea. "I do not write of the sea," he said, "I write of men who happened to have been on the sea." It should be added that it is the willingness to live hard and dangerously rather than the determination to collect adventure which yields rich results. Expeditions to get material for writing, like love affairs to learn of love, seldom make good literature. You cannot win the Muse by assault, although you may lose her by timorousness or lethargy. The interesting writer has an interesting mind and has led an interesting life (though perhaps uneventful to the outward eye), because he is interested in living. What could be less exciting than the visible life of Emily Dickinson immured in her respectable Amherst farm house? Yet there is nothing more exciting in American literature than some of her poetry!

In brief, no one can write well unless he has something definite to say. No one can have something to say unless his intellect and emotions have been busy. The intellect grows by what it feeds upon; the emotions enrich by exercise. It is unfortunately necessary to think, study, learn, and live hard and either deeply or extensively or both, before writing can be much more than practice. Every one knows that this is true, but few remember it, and still fewer plot their way accordingly. That is why there are one hundred facile clickers of the typewriter in this country for one real writer.

At this point the discussion may leave the metaphysics of writing and come down to actual practice. Given an idea (such as Keyserling's, that the American is in danger of an easy and attractive success on a low plane of culture), and with it a texture of knowledge and experience, what happens next in the process of good writing?

UNFOLDING AN IDEA

Bad writing may be due to a bad idea, or it may be due to a failure in expression that comes from bad thinking or bad English or both. If the idea is bad, nothing can be done except burn the manuscript and discourage the writer from inflicting more wandering words upon a society already written and talked to the point of distraction. If the English is defective, there are remedies, of which more later. But it is a safe guess that nine-tenths of the writing which honestly tries to be good and fails is spoiled in the fateful thinking between the birth of an idea and the setting down of the first word—in the moments of actual composition. Do not be deceived. Composition takes place before writing, even with those adepts who speak or write "without preparation." Their sub-consciousness is ready if they are not. They have caught the first link of the chain of unwinding thought and feel what is to come even if they do not yet know, consciously, what they are to say. If they are not so prepared, the expected happens—what editor does not know the hastily written article that changes from thought to padding halfway through, what audience is not familiar with the lecturer who relapses into wind and anecdote after the first fifteen minutes!

Every rhetoric treats—and many of them treat well—of this development of the idea which has so much to do with the success of that process by which good ideas are made communicable. The difficulty is that writers remember the directions in these books but fail to see the application of arid sets of rules to their living material.

I am desirous not to repeat from these books what logic requires of all who would unfold their minds, but rather to touch the actual moment of composition itself and show logic at work. And indeed it is impossible to begin or to end any discussion of writing with logic alone. This is where the textbook fails which takes a syllogism or an outline from the context of imagination and interest and exhibits it as a process that, abstracted from its element, is as unnatural as a dead trout on a sand bank.

Rather let us work by illustration, choosing a specific instance where logic and all else that helps to unfold an idea can be seen at work. I choose, because of the skill and flexibility involved, an editorial for a metropolitan paper, let us say an editorial on Prohibition, the theme of which has been determined in an editorial conference on a Tuesday noon, the editorial to be written by six of the same day.

The discussion in the conference of editorial writers ranged over the question as to whether Prohibition was justified by its fruits. The editor who took the assignment thought it was not, and the opposition to his opinion in the conference stirred his energies and quickened his mind. The idea which came to him as they talked was that nothing which happens to the present generation is of importance by comparison with what our children may find waiting for them when they come of age, and he argued that they would find a new crime and abundant means of committing it. This was his idea. It was born in the midst of the discussion because of opinion and experience already present in his mind but never so definitely embodied.

The conference breaks up and he goes back to his office to write. At first he spins his mind about the subject. Logic, the application of reason, is his first servant. What *are* the fruits of Prohibition? How can they be weighed? If a new crime is worse than an old evil, how can that be demonstrated? In such a chain of argument what comes first, and what shall follow it? His mind is clear and reasonable or he would not be a professional writer of editorials, and, willy-nilly, no matter how passionately he is devoted to proving his point, he will analyze his subject, consider cause and effect, order and balance, pro and con. A trained mind will complete its logicizing quickly; an untrained will often dodge the whole process and land in the dumps. But, short or long, no writing is safe without it. You must be sure of your grounds, clear as to your facts, reasonable in narrative or exposition or arguments. And yet the judicial mind is no guarantee of successful authorship. The best of reasoning will not assure the success of an editorial.

To return to the editor's office, imagination next begins to function, if indeed there is a "next" in so flashing a process as composition where, as in a sleight of hand, several operations may go on at once. Logic at the most merely shows what can and what cannot be done, not what is most expedient to do. The writer might analyze the fruits of Prohibition until the presses rusted without making an editorial, if logic only were at work.

In books on writing, imagination is discussed as something esoteric, possessed only by the great. Nonsense! There is not a step in elementary thinking where imagination does not guide. Imagination brings before the editorial writer pictures of possible attitudes. Imagination plays with possible beginnings and endings, selecting the best in the light of the effect he desires. It guides his thinking. Logic is the machine; imagination is the driver planning the course which he wants his car of thought to follow. If it cannot, if logic will not go that way, imagination must give way. In practice it does not by any means give way, and a good two-thirds of the political editorials which are inflicted upon a gullible public follow the warm imagination or the hidden desires of the writer, and let logic and truth go hang. Such writing is often skillful, but it is seldom in any sense good.

Next, intuition steps in. Intuition, which is only imagination in its sympathetic mood, warns the writer that cold logic will never persuade the Prohibitionist. It feels the mood of his audience and discards this excellent argument because of the prejudice it will arouse and chooses another because of associations favorable to the cause. Imagination and intuition have given him his strategy, logic has perfected his tactics. The preparation for this editorial campaign has taken perhaps fifteen minutes of concentrated thinking—*not* upon logic, imagination, rules, procedure, but upon the *subject,* with the editor's mind approaching it freely and by every method, concerned not with *how* he should think it out, but with thinking it out. Then, if he is a novice, he makes a plan, if he is a professional he jots down a note or two, or, without that, begins to write.

And thus in all writing, from a novel to a dictated letter, factors, complex in analysis but simple in operation, play and interplay. Be illogical, fail to see the relation of cause and effect, be disorderly in thinking, and you pay the price in muddled plots or muddy letters. Suppress your imagination, and your whole effort is unguided; you lack point, you are dull. As for intuition—that, like a well-favored countenance, comes by fortune. Be happy if you possess it.

The simple truth is that any one intelligent enough to put together complicated sentences will exercise whatever imagination and logic he possesses if at the moment of composition he feels the necessity for clear and directed thinking, which means, if he has grasped warmly a good idea. No elaborate rhetorical methods of plan and syllogism will help the lazy-minded. An eager brain will speed in a minute of thinking through logical processes that would take, literally, hours to analyze. Thinking must be learned while thinking; imagination developed by an attempt to shape experience. The important advice for the writer is, that, having grasped his idea, he must at the moment of composition begin to unfold it by the best way he can find.

WRITING IT OUT

What is the best way? The advice so far given has had much to say of ideas and thinking and very little of rules and specific directions, and may seem to the reader who has not put many years of writing behind him to be abstract, and perhaps, to use a damning term, academic. On the contrary, it is the textbooks which tell what kind of sentences to use, what kind of plots to seek, what kind of outlines to construct, that are academic for a writer past the preliminary stages. When you leave practice and begin to write because you have something to say, it is your thinking, not your memory of sentence structure, that needs jogging. No one actually writes by thinking of how to write sentences and paragraphs; a man writes well by thinking well of the thing to be written. The finest lecture on composition in my own experience was not a lecture at all but a description by Joseph Conrad of how he wrote *Victory*, a painfully difficult account of his glimpse of the girl heroine in one corner of the world and his knowledge of the man hero in another, and how he brought them together in his imagination to make the idea of the book, working with sweat and agony and delight to get into words the results of the situation in which he placed them. Beside such an account an analysis of the plot structure of a novel is cold and dead, no matter how much interest it may have as pure criticism. Writing at the moment of accomplishment is always synthetic; it builds up. You cannot write as an unpracticed foreigner tries to speak a foreign language, thinking of one word at a time.

And I repeat, that a description of the processes of writing is likely to be of more use to the author than specific rules for composition. For there is no such thing as a typical piece of exposition or narrative except in the most conventional modes, and therefore no one best and standardized way of writing. Every subject for writing brings its especial problems with it. There is no best way to write a short story, although unquestionably a best way for *your* particular story. Let us get down to concrete instances, then, in this discussion by descriptions rather than commands. You have an idea, felt strongly, seen clearly. What happens next?

What happens next depends upon the technique used by the writer, and technique is merely a trade name for the shrewdness with which your mind works out the idea as composing proceeds. (Technique is shrewdness. It is not a question of logic; it is how you use logic. It is not a question of imagination; it is how you use imagination.)

There is some excellent writing in Margaret Kennedy's *The Constant Nymph* which illustrates a technique that is not cold and formal but alive and challenging. The problem there was to say to the reader that Florence, the so apparently conventional English girl, who was to marry the half-brutal genius, Lewis Dodd, had the temperament, overlaid but alive in her brain, of her Aunt Evelyn, who ran away from good society with the great musician, Sanger, and was happy somehow in spite of cruel hardships manifold. Florence could faintly imagine falling in love with a mad musician, but Evelyn's folly seemed to her incredible. How then was the novelist to make it clear that she *was* like Evelyn, in spite of every apparent difference in taste and life, how was she to say it without bluntly announcing a fact which existed only in possibility at the beginning of the novel, and so destroying the sense of reality of her narrative. Read pp. 83-93 of *The Constant Nymph* and see what technique means—

She remembered her aunt very well. Nobody who had known the brilliant creature before her sudden and complete disappearance could possibly forget her. . . . She left vivid impressions of laughter and excitement and people crowding round to hear what she said. . . . Florence was sometimes told that she resembled her aunt, but she could not feel it herself. . . . But she lacked that overwhelming power to charm which Evelyn had possessed independently, as it were, from all her other qualities. . . .

"Poor Evelyn! Poor girl!" muttered Charles into his coffee cup. "That fellow was a brute."

"I expect," said Florence aggressively, "that she got a little bored with polite society. The world's a big place. . . ."

As she sauntered along Chesterton Lane, lugging her unwieldy 'cello and nodding to acquaintances, she thought curiously about her aunt, and wondered if it was just mere boredom which had prompted her to fling her bonnet so effectually over the mill. . . . Had there been a force more potent than mere discontent? . . . To her it was clear that Evelyn had been happy, content in the life she had chosen, finding romance in it perhaps—a splendid quality, dark and violent and exciting, like a Russian novel. . . .

Then Lewis Dodd writes brusquely that Evelyn's children need help—

"Really, sir [she said to her father], I think . . . you are prejudiced because of Aunt Evelyn. . . . I often wonder why you take it so for granted that she was miserable. We can't know. That sort of life is attractive to some people. There is something rather fine, when you come to think of it, about an uncompromising demand for freedom. Our life is, in a way, so cramped. . . ."

And so she goes to the Tyrol, and everything subtly prophesied in this introduction, from which I have quoted only significant sentences, happens as it was possible for it to happen, given that delicate conjunction of circumstances which the novelist in pursuit of life for her story proposes to arrange. Such a preparation, such a handling of material, is the quality which I have somewhat crudely called shrewdness. It is technique in action. The imagination of the novelist conceived of nature about to repeat her work of transformation in this prim Florence, and shrewdness devised the way in which it should be told.

Technique involves the same foresight, if less imagination and less shrewdness, in simpler matters such as writing an editorial, handling the theme for a scientific paper, preparing a speech, or writing a short story. The good writer keeps his idea in hand as he writes, expanding it slowly, often painfully, as his

imagination runs ahead, or his intellect tests its sound-
ness, but always keeping it in hand, even if, like an
oriental talisman, it changes shape and appearance as
the double process of clarification and expansion goes
on. He does not think, "I shall begin with the known
and go to the unknown" (which is one familiar device
of technique). Instead, with his mind on his idea he
seeks the best way to unroll *that idea*, and his success
depends upon his shrewdness as much as upon the excellence of his thought.

What, if any, are the practical benefits to be gained
from thinking of writing as a process like this? Not,
to be sure, any rules that can be stored in the back
of the mind—where they will probably remain until,
as a finished writer, one is asked, not to write, but to
teach writing to others; but certainly the only approach to writing that can be helpful in practice as
well as in theory. For whoever tries to *find* a pattern
to fit his ideas, instead of *following* a ready-made one,
will be likely to seek the best possible expression of
which he is capable.

The monotony of the current short story in America
is not so much due to lack of inspiration in its writers,
or the superficiality of American life, as to the set
form in which the material is arranged in order to
lead to a definite climax. Imagination is fettered by
a conventional method, and shrewdness is sacrificed
to safety. It is a case of secondhand technique. If
the characters refuse in reality to act as they should

in a successful short story, why jazz the reality or sentimentalize it! Such a writing by formula corrupts good writing and corrupts the taste for good writing, as is shown by the praise which teachers give to mechanically perfect and thoroughly artificial stories. If such stories sell easily because they are easy to read, they would sell quite as easily and be far better reading if they were written with more freedom and freshness. "Playing safe," which is the essence of most short-story courses, is even more fatal, sooner or later, in writing than elsewhere.

CONCLUSION OF THIS CHAPTER

If you do not write well, or if you find it impossible to make others think that you write well, the first area to investigate is your own mind and the ideas afloat there. The first question is not, are the ideas good or bad? Reverse that inquisition. Ask rather whether they are formed or unformed, interesting or uninteresting to you. And of those which you are using for writing—ideas for stories, articles, books—ask, are they ordered or disordered, full-blown or pinched halfway like a frosted cornstalk?

An excellent test of mental condition is a lecture or any kind of informal talk. Do you stick fast in the middle? Do you hop from point to point? Do you ramble? Do you get nowhere finally? It is a common experience, and, discounting shyness and the normal difficulties of speaking, an excellent way to diagnose your ills.

A lecture should not be read, it should be talked. Therefore it comes closer to the actual process of the mind laboring in composition than writing, which can be seen and revised as you proceed. A lecture once begun must be finished. Now a good lecturer should be able to see his talk as a whole in half a dozen topics expressed in a sentence each and leading one out of the other. His mind runs on the track of these sentences as he talks to his audience, and they hold his developing idea aloft and coherent while he expands his thought in words. Thus a paragraph of notes should represent concretely the gist of an hour's lecture, and this paragraph will infallibly keep the speaker to his subject and guarantee that he goes through all of it, *provided* these few sentences are the guideposts of the way in which his mind has already traveled. The quaint story of the theologian, Jonathan Edwards, who on his day-long rides through the Berkshire wilderness followed long trains of dogmatic reasoning and literally pinned the conclusion of each in a sentence to his saddle bow, illustrates the method.

To get the *précis* of a long talk into a paragraph which has the power to promote instant expansion of the thought in words, the lecturer must first have built up and out his prime idea into a fabric so elaborate that to talk it all might take two hours instead of one. Then he has pruned and trimmed it. Finally, he has reduced

it all back again to essential ideas which now represent
in simplest form the results of his thinking. If he has
the material the topics call for, his few resulting sentences will be good for an hour's talk anywhere, any
time, until the ideas grow stale, his interest flags, and
that lecture is best tossed into the waste basket. All
this if his mind is functioning as it should. If it is
not, the attempt to lecture will find it out.

Yet no technical method is good unless the ideas
themselves are good. The excellence of anything must
depend upon the quality of thought as well as upon
the method of thinking. There are passages of formal
poetry in the less inventive end of the eighteenth century which for lucidity and logic can scarcely be ex-
celled, and yet mean nothing of any interest or significance. So it is with all writing. The journalist
is too often an adept at the skillful development of a
worthless idea. Out of almost nothing he can make
what seems to be something. He knows how to make
a "story" when there is really nothing to tell, how to
write an editorial every day when there are only four
good topics a week. His profession has suffered in
general estimation from the vices of its less principled
members.

The most exquisite logic in the world cannot make
a writer even sensible if he has no sense of what is
true and what is not. You cannot, in more familiar
words, make a silk purse from a sow's ear, or wise
writing out of unwisdom and ignorance, or good

writing by mere facile cleverness. Yet it is useful to know how to make a purse even if it is better to go elsewhere for your material. Education and experience must supply the material, without which the counsel given in this book is worse than useless. To teach how to write where there is nothing useful to say is the eighth deadly sin—for which many a sinner will, one hopes, some day get adequate punishment. The writer makes his own mind as well as he can, and lives his own life as richly as he is able. Then what he learns of writing is of some use.

Chapter IV

HOW TO SAY IT

Books upon writing usually begin with an imaginative picture of a writer charged with ideas and with pen in hand or fingers poised over the typewriter. He is ready to write, but the words will not come. With the picture is the caption, "Study Section XXVII on paragraph structure."

Something is wrong with that picture, or with the caption. As I have endeavored to explain, if the writer is *ready* to write, he can write through to the end regardless of rules for paragraph and sentence structure, even though he may bump and jerk like a rider on his first horseback ride. If he is really ready the idea has taken form in his mind and has developed outlines and subdivisions. It is impossible for him to stick fast except in the attempt to get the right turn of a phrase, or the necessary word, or because his memory fails him. Readiness to write means that you know what you want to say, though by no means necessarily just how you will phrase or refine it. Readiness to write means also that you are in no danger of blurting out your story naïvely. You know what is to come first because you see what must come last.

And yet the picture of the helpless author who is ready to write in this sense, and yet unable to express himself, has plenty of originals. The writer is like a dynamo which, run smoothly as it may, must have wires to transmit its energy. The wires in this case are the niceties of language. Ideas and their developments must be translated into English words. Are they not in words already as they form in the mind? Only occasionally and then incompletely phrased, although a sentence may jump into the mind as you think. Ideas are more resemblant to pictures, the significance of which one feels, than to paragraphs of statement. They must be worded.

This finding of the right sentences, right phrases, right terms, right words, is not a question of style. That comes later. It is the simpler problem of how to get words and link them together. A child may profit by an analysis of language structure—grammar, syntax, rhetoric. But for a mature writer to approach from this end is to be lost. He is not studying language, he is trying to express; and for him a word is not a grammatical unit, it is a name for what he is thinking, and a sentence is the explanation thereof. If he cannot handle English grammar let him drop writing and go back to exercises. His business as a writer is to study, not rhetoric, but his thought, and to grope for the final answer in the linking together of suitable words. And it is the increasing determination to say it right which makes the good writer.

The actual process is much too complicated to analyze completely even if it were worth while to analyze it, for of course getting the right words reacts upon thinking and helps the development of the idea. Put such subtleties aside and observe the moment when the fingers are poised upon the typewriter, ready. Then the brain is furiously at work to find the instruments of expression for what is already clear in outline to the mind. The instrument of expression for an actor might be pantomime, for a musician, harmonies of sound; but for the writer it is words that he needs, and an arrangement of words that will catch his meaning exactly.

He must try until he gets what he wants—that is the only honest advice to give to a reasonably mature writer. If he is weak in vocabulary he will not succeed. In that case he needs more reading. If sentences will not flow and adjust themselves to his thought, he will not succeed. In this case he needs, presumably, more reading again to make familiar the weave and pattern of his own tongue. If he cannot get what he wants do not teach him more about writing. Do not teach him writing at all. Give him knowledge, experience, intimacy with expressed ideas. Educate him. He is not ready to write.

Of course, no one is ever completely educated, and no one finds words waiting always upon the tip of the mind. There is always difficulty in expression except in warm and favored moments. Judge for yourself

whether this difficulty comes from insufficient training, from the normal disabilities of every mind, from
laziness, or from a third cause, not yet discussed, ignorance as to what good writing requires.

The American novel is just now in a flourishing
condition—especially the American realistic novel,
which is written with great seriousness, usually about
a youth trying to escape from the dull standardization
of so much American life. The midwestern novel of
the farm is a good example. Scores of such novels
have been published, yet, with few exceptions, they
read as if one indefatigable hand had written them all.
The themes are clear, the technique not bad, but there
is no distinction in the writing because there is no
attempt at careful expression. The honest writers
chose the first words that came handy, and set them
down in any way which adequately (not excellently)
expressed their meaning.

Yet every one of these novels differed from every
other one in at least three ways: the characters were
different, the background was different, the temperament and personality of the author were different. No
one of these books was rightly written so long as the
forms of expression used in it would have done just
as well for any other. It is not yet the question of
style that I am discussing, although I am on its
borders. It is the simpler problem of the right word,
the most expressive clause. And for these novelists,
and for all writers, the will to get the best expression,

and to get it the first time, not waiting for the revision which is coming later, would be worth an infinite study of technique—provided always that these authors knew from experience what good writing was like. (The desire to be right will quickly enlarge the knowledge of the means of expression as one finds them in good examples of English: without that will, one may read a lifetime without being able to write, may write for a lifetime without attaining distinction.)

The current short story in America, which has become a stereotyped affair produced in vast quantities by a skillful but artificial technique, is instructive also. The choice of words is as careful in the short story as it is slipshod in the realistic novel. Short stories, according to current convention, must be vivid, and the writer knows that he must get vivid words, which means usually that he must get words that carry the full force of his idea. (Often he overstrains and explodes into fireworks of adjectives and adverbs which conceal the picture in a cloud of sparks.)

There is no such compulsion, however, upon sentences or paragraphs in the short story, beyond a certain speed of movement supposed to be essential. Therefore a staccato structure, and a conventional overemphasis, inherited from Dickens and Bret Harte and Kipling, have become what may be called the short-story style. The writer strains to exhaust the resources of vocabulary; then lets his words drop into molds as commonplace as those which turn out type

or metal toys. Admirable plot ideas, like those of
O. Henry for example, are by this process put into a
language that already is growing stale, since the words
strain for the verity of the moment and the rhythm is
that of other men, or is no rhythm at all:

Capitalize it, friend typo—that last word—word of words
in the epiphany of life and love. The scent of the flowers,
the booty of the bee, the primal drip of spring waters, the
overture of the lark, the twist of lemon peel on the cocktail
of creation—such is the bride. Holy is the wife; revered the
mother; galliptious is the summer girl—but the bride is the
certified check among the wedding presents that the gods send
in when man is married to mortality.

The car glided up the Golden Way. On the bridge of the
great cruiser the captain stood, trumpeting the sights of the
big city to his passengers. Wide-mouthed and open-eared,
they heard the sights of the metropolis thundered forth to
their eyes. Confused, delirious with excitement and provincial
longings, they tried to make ocular responses to the mega-
phonic ritual. In the solemn spires of spreading cathedrals
they saw the home of the Vanderbilts; in the busy bulk of
the Grand Central depot they viewed, wonderingly, the frugal
cot of Russell Sage. Bidden to observe the highlands of the
Hudson, they gaped, unsuspecting, at the upturned moun-
tains of a new-laid sewer. To many the elevated railroad
was the Rialto, on the stations of which uniformed men sat
and made chop suey of your tickets. And to this day in
the outlying districts many have it that Chuck Connors, with
his hand on his heart, leads reform; and that, but for the
noble municipal efforts of one Parkhurst, a district attorney,

the notorious "Bishop" Potter gang would have destroyed law and order from the Bowery to the Harlem river.

Expression is the transmission of the automobile. It is worthless without dynamic ideas behind; but they fail to go anywhere or do anything when deprived of it. Good ideas, of course, make for good expression, and, to speak accurately, are developed and perfected by means of it. Three-quarters of the job of expression, roughly speaking, is accomplished in that mental shaping of the idea which largely precedes writing and which we call composition. But the other quarter covers the whole province of the choice of words and constitutes the chief practicing ground of the beginning writer. It *is,* in fact, writing.

There are two schools of advice as to the perfecting of expression. The first says, write quickly while the mind is warm and revise afterward. The second insists that no words should be written down until they are right. Teachers of writing seem to favor the first; writers, I believe, in general, practice the second. Once a phrase is crystallized, they say, the life of the idea behind it passes into words and is never again fluid. Therefore it is best never to let a sentence crystallize on paper until it says exactly what you want, or what at the moment you think you want. It is better to stop and walk around the table or around the block until the right words come (as they usually will with the aid of the subconsciousness) than to go on warmly with the promise of revision later. I be-

lieve myself in "get it right the very first time," or at
least as near right as one can. Flushed writing, done
in a fine fervor at midnight, when the imagination runs
far ahead of the words, is flat reading usually the next
morning, although if good writing does come fast,
thank Heaven, and preserve it. The time to say what
you mean is when you are first saying it.

Not that one discards revision. No idea comes perfect at even the most laborious birth. *Nothing should
ever be published without at least one revision* in which
the final kinks come out and the hidden ambiguities
disappear. But such a revision as one sees in composition books where the text is corrected on the
margin or between the lines is the worst kind, at least
at the beginning. Do not revise in this sense; *rewrite.*
As one writes through again, using the first manuscript of course, but not copying, taking a sentence in
the eye and then freely rewriting it, the ideas behind
move once more with some of their original freedom,
and the changes inevitably made are in harmony with
the theme as well as with rules for correctness in
diction. In such a rewriting alterations are made unconsciously as well as consciously, and the changes
in word order or word choice, which should be slight
if you have done your first job well, represent a closer
fitting of expression to thought. It is like the second
fitting of a suit of clothes, where the tailor's trained
fingers make nice adjustments for reasons not always
clear even to him.

There are admirable instances in Keats and Tennyson, both ardent and successful revisers. The latter's song in *The Princess*—

> Thy voice is heard thro' rolling drums
>> That beat to battle where he stands;
> Thy face across his fancy comes,
>> And gives the battle to his hands.
> A moment, while the trumpets blow,
>> He sees his brood about thy knee;
> The next, like fire he meets the foe,
>> And strikes him dead for thine and thee.

was originally—

> Lady, let the rolling drums
> Beat to battle where thy warrior stands:
> Now thy face across his fancy comes,
>> And gives the battle to his hands.

> Lady, let the trumpets blow,
> Clasp thy little babes about thy knee:
> Now their warrior father meets the foe,
>> And strikes him dead for thine and thee.

Nor is it to be forgotten that Keats in revision changed "low-brow'd" to "deep-brow'd" in his famous line "That deep-brow'd Homer ruled as his demesne." A final and most illuminating example has already been cited for other purposes by Professor C. Alphonso Smith.

It is the comparison between the conclusion which Seward suggested for Lincoln's First Inaugural Address—

I close. We are not, we must not be, aliens or enemies, but fellow-countrymen and brethren. Although passion has strained our bonds of affection too hardly, they must not, I am sure they will not, be broken. The mystic chords which, proceeding from so many battlefields and so many patriot graves, pass through all the hearts and all hearths in this broad continent of ours, will yet again harmonize in their ancient music when breathed upon by the guardian angel of the nation.

and the conclusion as Lincoln delivered it after careful rewriting—

I am loath to close. We are not enemies, but friends. We must not be enemies. Though passion may have strained, it must not break, our bonds of affection. The mystic chords of memory, stretching from every battlefield and patriot grave to every living heart and hearthstone all over this broad land, will yet swell the chorus of the Union when again touched, as surely they will be, by the better angels of our nature.

And last of all, when you have rewritten, then revise again your manuscript by rereading it and correcting it. There will be plenty left to do; and if it is rewriting which makes good writing, it is final, careful correction that insures accuracy and cuts down printers' bills.

Chapter V

STYLE

STYLE is like happiness. Every one recognizes it, every one describes it, but no two people agree as to its exact nature. Indeed, literary style has been discussed so often as the rare and fine flower of perfect writing that there is a common belief that style is like a top hat, something every one may like to possess but can very well do without. Style in its more exquisite forms is, it is true, rare, and so is exquisite writing. But style as an accompaniment of good writing is not a grace superadded to what does well enough without it, but a part of excellence itself. It is not a cause but a result of good writing, and is no more beyond the reach of the aspirant than clearness or force. Who does not attempt to form a style, does not try to write as well as his subject demands and his intellect permits.

False ideas of style spring generally from the belief that literary style is an ornament, a something put on to composition by a final polish after expression is complete. Unfortunately, too much of what is called "literary" writing supports this vicious theory. One of the most popular poems ever written was Sir Walter Scott's "Lady of the Lake." Scott as a story-teller

was a great artist, and when his narrative moves to
the view halloo the style is inseparable from the lively
verse—

> Yelled on the view the opening pack;
> Rock, glen, and cavern paid them back,
>
> . . . . .
>
> Clattered a hundred steeds along,
> Their peal the merry horns rung out
> A hundred voices joined the shout.

But the unwilling child who is given the poem to read
as an assignment for classroom work, early encounters
such a passage as this—

> Now back they wend their watery way,
> And, "O my sire!" did Ellen say,
> "Why urge thy chase so far astray?
> And why so late returned? And why—"
> The rest was in her speaking eye.
> "My child, the chase I follow far,
> 'Tis mimicry of noble war;
> And with that gallant pastime reft
> Were all of Douglas I have left."

He feels it to be overworded, and it is, with this
amendment, that fine words already stale are put in to
adorn what should have been an unchecked narrative.
This is not Scott's style; it is his rhetoric.

Style is not ornament. To define it positively is

not so easy. Buffon asserted that order and movement were two of its chief attributes. Perhaps the simplest and most inclusive account of it, is to say that style is the measure of control over what is being written. The control itself comes from a firm handling of the idea and a mastery of expression, but when power over the order of thought and of words, and over words themselves, approaches completeness the result is felt as a perfection and harmony of the whole. That measure of completeness is style. There is an exact equivalence between the style of an able writer and the style of an accomplished golfer or a perfect oarsman. It is not what they do that gives them style, but how they do it and the effect of their doing. Thus style *is* beauty—but not the beauty of prettiness. Its beauty is akin to the beauty of architecture where a steel structure of most uncompromising lines has a beauty of its own, the same in cause as the beauty of the Taj Mahal though so different in effect.

If I am right, style is a possibility for every writer and a necessity for every really good writer. It is the result of a good job, and in fact is bound to come if the art of expression discussed in the last chapter is carried to perfection. Indeed it is well known that the simple letters of Lincoln or the even simpler pages of Defoe have style precisely as have the elaborate sonnets of Shakespeare. Immature writing, slovenly writing, bad writing, or good enough writing, has no style, chiefly because it is unfinished. There was style in the trenchant phrases of Wilson's war notes; indeed, it was the intense expressiveness of their style which angered those who did not agree with the ideas expressed. There was no style in the ornate panegyrics hastily composed for the press at the time of his death.

Style of a sort is possible for every honest writer, and he must get his own style if he is ever to be effective. But fineness of style, especially in the choice and disposition of words and in the harmonies of diction, is possible only for the fine nature. A literary style is quite as impossible for the unliterary as excellent music for the man without an ear. This is one difference between the necessity for accurate expression discussed in the last chapter and the desirability of an excellent and personal style. The distinction is important, and disregard of it has produced a race of would-be literary writers who learn to imitate a great style badly when they might develop an honest, if modest, style of their own. Dr. Johnson's advice to sit up nights with Addison never meant that to write like Addison was desirable for every man. Models may be necessary at the beginning in order to know what can be done, although it is far better to read them, not as models of style, but as good reading; nevertheless, style is the result of saying what has to be said as well as it can be said by you in your own way. Here one can expect success without being either Addison or Shakespeare.

I have written so far without mention of personality. Ever since Buffon was made against his plain intention to define style as the man himself, it has been urged that style is really the personality of the author molding expression. The truth is, of course, that every piece of good writing has in it all that a writer possesses, including his personality. Personality does not make style, but naturally it gets into it; or, to put it differently, only when expression reaches the pitch of style can personality get into words. Without strong personality many kinds of excellent writing are possible, but never perhaps what is called literature, and never, quite certainly, a strongly marked style. The literary writers, who are creatures of strong personality without exception, stamp their style with personality as well as with other qualities, and one can tell in an instant that Conrad wrote these sentences:

Singleton stood at the door with his face to the light and his back to the darkness. And alone in the dim emptiness of the sleeping forecastle he appeared bigger, colossal, very old; old as Father Time himself, who should have come there into this place as quiet as a sepulchre to contemplate with patient eyes the short victory of sleep, the consoler.

and Kipling this one:

It is written in the chronicles of the Satpura Bhils together with many other matters not fit for print, that through

five days after the day that he had put his mark upon them,
Jan Chinn the First hunted for his people; and on the five
nights of those days the tribe was gloriously and entirely
drunk.

Indeed, excess of personality may most unpleasantly
impress itself upon style (as W. C. Brownell in his
book on style has said) with disagreeable mannerisms
as a result. See, for example, Dickens at his sentimental worst, or Carlyle:

And yet this Rousseau, as we say, with his passionate ap-
peals to mothers, with his *Contrat-social*, with his celebra-
tions of nature, even of savage life in nature, did once more
touch upon Reality, struggle towards Reality; was doing the
function of a Prophet to his Time. As *he* could, and as the
Time could!

I choose writers of an earlier period because the
mannerisms of our contemporaries (Cabell, for example, Chesterton, or Virginia Woolf) are sprightly
until we tire of them.

The less one thinks of one's unique personality the
better, when it comes to writing. If you have one,
and acquire a style, your personality will go over into
your writing; if you have not, it will not; and to
borrow personality by imitating another's mannerisms
is a sure path to failure. It is hard enough to acquire that balance and rhythm and exactness of word
meaning which makes a piece of writing a perfect

mirror of both yourself and your thought. To try to make writing express what you are not and have not is folly.

Nor are we concerned here with styles in the sense in which that word is often used. There are the styles of various periods of literary history, and there are various styles, the grave, the flippant, the pointed, the gay, adapted to various moods and subjects. Yet, clearly, if you begin with your own firmly handled idea and write as well as you can to the point of reaching style in your performance, the kind of style will take care of itself.

One word of caution. It is wise, as is suggested elsewhere, to suspect fluency and warmth in writing. When you think that you are writing finely, what you have written is very likely to prove rhetoric. Suspect the style you are proud of. If your education has been that common to thousands of Americans, you have been drilled in imitation. When the words flow along an easy pattern and gorgeous phrases mold themselves in your mind, there is more than a chance that you are subconsciously remembering how some one else wrote a story or described a scene. It takes more than the reading of a textbook and a year's writing to find a style of your own.

CHAPTER VI

MECHANICS

WILL the writer who both feels and knows what he wants to say, write accurately? Will his expression be as correct as it is fluent? If the thinking and feeling are right, will the grammar and other mechanics of writing take care of themselves?

Answer these questions by another one. If the owner of an automobile understands his engine and knows where he wants to go, will he therefore and thereby be able to drive his car with safety to the car and himself? The reply, naturally, is that if he wants to drive and has an automobile, he can be trusted to learn to steer and to shift gears, and to learn to do so quickly. So it is with grammar, punctuation, and the elements of rhetoric.

GRAMMAR

I will not enter into the vexed problem of how much formal grammar children should be taught. This book is not for children, and it is certain that its readers already possess more of the grammar of their own tongue than the best educated foreigner. The difficulties for would-be writers seldom lie in grammar, except in the rare case of a cowboy poet, or a talented story-teller who has heard nothing but bad grammar in his youth. Even then, learning to write with fair grammatical accuracy is the least of his troubles. The real stir over grammar is not about the principal parts of verbs, or even the case of the relative pronoun, but over issues created by ignorant, pedantic, or self-distrustful writers.

The real problem is how to master the niceties of English grammar, which means, in plain English, how to convey the subtler thoughts by a word form and a word order that adequately convey them. But there are, as it happens, few niceties in English grammar. A writer with brains enough to write ten consecutive pages, a writer with a brain structure capable of composing a good business letter, needs only to have the existence of the subjunctive, the vagaries of the relative, the shifts of "shall" and "will," and a half-dozen other niceties called to his attention in order to use them when he needs to do so. Slovenly grammar, a sentence inexpressive because an inaccuracy in syntax blurs the exactness of meaning, is too common, but can be corrected more readily than a bad taste in neckties. "Was" where "were" gives the exact shade of meaning in a statement contrary to fact, "should" instead of "would," a participial clause or phrase modifying the wrong noun, are precisely as common as slovenly pronunciation and bad table manners. A writer who really desires to write well will assuredly correct them of his own motion. All he needs is to be told that he is slipshod, and to be referred to a manual. And bad grammar of the simpler sort, "done" for "did," "her" for "she," scarcely enters into the writer's problem at all. In short, all that is required is precisely the same desire for good grammar that most of us have for clean faces. Not to have what little there is of English grammar at your command (even if you remember not three rules) is as disgraceful as a typhus epidemic in a civilized city.

It would be fortunate if more concern were given to these niceties of grammar which pin language to your meaning, and less to disputed questions of usage. "He don't" and "it is me" and "different than" are wrong in logic of course, but usage may yet confirm the first two as permitted idioms, and the British have adopted wholesale "different to," which is quite as indefensible logically as the third. A fastidious writer will always be conservative in such choices and hold to exactness in his expression; yet let it be remembered and repeated, that no matter what all the school teachers and all the textbooks may say, a colloquialism, such as "he don't" is venal beside a clumsy, obscure phrasing which actually conceals thought.

Our grammar has reached its present simplicity by a series of ungrammatical colloquialisms which have been sanctioned finally because they were convenient. It was the frightful grammatical errors of the illiterate

English in the Norman-French period that saved us from the awkward complexities of Anglo-Saxon. Historically, "you" in the singular, and "its" however used, are quite as ungrammatical as "he don't." They are accepted: the latter is not—yet. The eighteenth century grammarians made many of our rules by analogy with Latin, disregarding too often the authority of the best usage of the times.

Follow the best writers and listen to the best speakers. If you are in doubt consult a good textbook, and if you doubt that, compare its rules with the usage of writers you respect. But do not be persuaded that the question as to whether "had better" (a very useful colloquialism) is correct or not is as important as the ability to use the inflections of English for the perfect rendering of thought. It is the undisputed, not the disputed, usages that chiefly affect good writing. If a sentence is accurate and expressive it is, in English, usually grammatical. If it is expressive, and yet not grammatical, as in "Between you and I, there are many differences," good taste should defer to the expectations of the well read that the objective "me" shall follow the preposition. Yet if you write "I" for "me" you will not be so offensive to the spirit of the language as when you say, "Really to succeed is my desire," in the attempt not to split an infinitive which clearly needs splitting.[1]

[1] See, for instructive examples of infinitives which in English should be split, Tract No. 15 of the Society for Pure English. Oxford University Press, 1925.

RHETORIC, ALIVE AND DEAD

All this applies in principle to the broader questions of arrangement of words which we call rhetoric. Rhetoric is a dead thing unless it is re-created every time the author writes. In the words of Sentimental Tommy, he must always find a way. He can be taught Unity, Coherence, and Emphasis, and every complexity of sentence structure, yet all his knowledge will be worthless for writing unless the gathering thought employs these devices for much desired ends. The mature writer is not concerned with the study so much as with the use of rhetoric. If he still lacks self-confidence, let him return to his textbooks, and also read more widely in good English, but he cannot stop when he has memorized the ways of expression; his task is to master his own thought and learn how to express *it*.

Here is a simple experiment. Take a model paragraph, such as the rhetorics supply so abundantly—

The Rockies have neither the individuality nor the beauty of the Alps. They stretch in sweeping ranges where the single mountain is lost in the chain, and their forms are more rugged, their slopes more bare, their peaks less graceful, than the snowy Alpine summits which carry green meadows on their breasts and tower into single pinnacles. The Rockies expand the imagination, the Alps refine and heighten it.

The thought structure of this paragraph is simple. It has a topic sentence with two subtopics, "indi-

viduality" and "beauty." The next sentence expands
these topics by the use of detail. The third sentence
carries the thought one step further by showing the
result of what has been established. You will be advised to choose a simple topic of your own making and
write a new paragraph employing the same paragraph
structure.

This is an excellent way of learning how good writing is conducted, for if you follow the plan of the
Alpine paragraph you cannot fail to be clear and conclusive—and the more practice you get in such
mechanical labor when you are young the better for
your English in maturity. It is a step in learning
how to write, and the outlining of themes and practice in balanced or periodic sentences are other steps.
But this is not writing! Your paragraph will be as
dead as a salted herring, as all mechanical imitation
must be. It is a product of analysis, not synthesis.
No models, however excellent, can determine *your*
particular expression in a particular instance. Only
the nature of a living thought can do that.

After the writer has learned how others have told
stories, have written paragraphs, or have made plays,
the slate must be wiped clean, and real writing begun.
It is hard work, but the work does not go into studying how thought in general can be developed, it goes
into finding how *your* thought can be expressed, your
story told. There is a vast difference. The answer to
the first is in rhetorical terms such as climax, bal-

ance, coherence; the answer to the second is in concrete, living terms of a story, a paragraph, a conclusion. If a woman grows jealous of her daughter, what happens next? If we have sacrificed quality to quantity in American education, what is to be done about it? The writer, like the painter, has to keep his eye on his subject. The more technique he has the better, but the technique should come from wanting it. Real education in real writing comes from having to write, and trying to put everything you have into the writing.

I am not disparaging an education in rhetoric. Among Americans, especially, there are nine professional writers who show the results of too little discipline in analysis, for one who has been spoiled by too much teaching. Loose, ugly sentences and crippled paragraphs in the pages of an author whose imagination is worthy of better vehicles, are often symptoms of defective discipline. The guilty do not know the resources of their language, or have never been made critical of their own expression. Nevertheless, when you are graduated from rhetoric, put your textbooks on the shelf where you can reach them easily and study your subject—follow, not rules, but it.

FOSSIL RHETORIC

Rhetoric, which in itself is an almost indispensable tool for the writer, may indeed become a positive hindrance to writing. As long as it is alive we who write do not think of it as rhetoric; but if it becomes a set of rules to be consulted for each move in composition it is dead and an obstruction.

Furthermore, some rhetoric is not only dead, it is fossilized. Many textbooks carry arbitrary instructions which have no support in current usage and which cramp the innocent writer who adopts them like a too tight collar. "A paragraph should never begin with a conjunction." Why not? "A sentence should never end with a preposition." But sometimes that is incomparably the best way to end a sentence. "Paragraphs should contain a mixture of loose and periodic sentences." But this is like saying that a stroll should contain a pleasing variety of long and short steps! It all depends, naturally, upon the stroll or the subject of the paragraph.

The experienced writer will soon learn to test such rules, and all rules, first by the practice of good writers, which represents the fruits of experience, and next by expediency—do they help or hinder his own practice? He will find that the bulk of rhetorical principle is sound and helpful; he will find that he is never hampered by a rule that has sense and reason behind it.

HOW TO USE RHETORIC

A model illustration of what rhetoric does, and cannot do, is to be seen in the writing of paragraphs, to which reference has already been made. Slovenly, hit-or-miss writing, fluent but not cogent, is often due to a simple inability to write good paragraphs. Writers who are excellent in other respects break here. A close analysis of samples of current journalistic writing would expose hundreds of weak paragraphs, mere slices of a whole that are not units of thought at all, paragraphs that trail, bump, fade, or muddle, in which the sentences may be good enough.

What is the remedy? Suppose yourself to be deficient, as probably you are, in the nice art of the paragraph. Do you know what a paragraph is? If not, find out from the nearest rhetoric. Do you know how a paragraph is developed, held together, pointed? If not, find out by study. You are now equipped for self-analysis, which can be applied ruthlessly to your own paragraphs. And then, having revealed weaknesses, seen where the engine of thought has missed fire, observed how your mind has let go in the middle of a paragraph and never again pulled the sentences together—why, after a course in such paragraph analysis you may drop criticism and go back to writing, and this time have a better expectation of getting your thoughts in order and your sentences in hand. But keep the two processes of criticism and writing separate; *analyze paragraphs,* but when you write, *develop thought.*

Choose any one of the paragraphs of this book, and

discover by analysis and criticism whether the writer has been fortunate or unfortunate, cogent or careless in his handling of a unit of thought. It is admirable practice and may yield some harmless if malicious satisfaction. But to stop with such analysis is to learn rhetoric, not writing.

One mechanical device in paragraph writing stays more or less mechanical even when it is used in the processes of active thought. Transitional words, phrases, clauses, sentences, but especially transitional words like *but, however, and, yet, nevertheless,* are the signal flags of thinking, and it is hard to go wrong with the right ones rightly used, or, conversely, right with the wrong ones. They are the most useful words in the language for clearness and coherence and good aim in writing. Transitional terms cannot be forced into loose, badly composed writing. They are too definite for loose thinking. If you can change an *and* to a *but* without much damage, there is something wrong with your English. Substitute *ands* for *buts, howevers* for *in spite ofs,* in a good paragraph, and see what a mess is made of the thought. On the other hand, notice how the lazy paragraph on page 79, where this subject is further considered, is tightened and clarified by the use of the proper connectives. They show the weakness of sluggish thinking as rain water shows the low spots on a golf course. Take care of your *ands* and *buts* and the coherence of your paragraphs will take care of itself because you cannot get your connectives right until you have thought clearly.

PUNCTUATION

The same general principles apply to the mechanics of punctuation. There are definite rules for the science of punctuation, with logic behind them, and an obvious gain in clarity when they are observed. It is easy to learn them and easy to apply them. But punctuation is an art as well as a science. Whether a clause is nonrestrictive or restrictive and should be set off, or not set off, by a comma is a question of fact determined by the meaning of the sentence. One learns the distinction and, in good writing, invariably applies the rule. But whether a comma should set apart two independent clauses or they should go unpunctuated, or whether a semicolon should take the place of a comma between two independent clauses not closely connected, may depend upon such subtle matters as rhythm, your own style, and the kind of emphasis sought for the clauses in question. The same is true of so-called rhetorical punctuation where a comma may be set merely to indicate a pause in a long sentence. The science of punctuation can be readily learned, but the disputed usages are nearly always questions of art rather than science. Good practice results when the will to express your thought exactly and fully leads to the choice of the punctuation which without question accomplishes the desired ends.

Like rhetoric, the punctuation of many pretty good writers is slovenly in the extreme. They have not mastered the mechanics of punctuation. There is no excuse for not doing so, since a day of study should give the kind of writer who will be reading this book all the information he needs. But, this done, it is better for him to leave disputes over doubtful usage alone and proceed while writing to perfect his own art of punctuation, the punctuation which will bring out his meaning with absolute certainty. If he has the will and the power to write, and will think of punctuation as he thinks of rhetoric, namely, as a means of perfect expression, he need have little fear of breaking rules. The rules, he will find, were made for, not against, him.

CONCLUSION OF THIS CHAPTER

English has been magnificently developed by thirty generations of writers in poetry and prose, and, while new styles are certain, it is unlikely that there will be substantial additions to the mechanics of expression. Yet every writer, after he has learned what has been and what can be done, must traverse the historic process of creation again in the pursuit of his own especial purposes. He must make his own rhetoric, or what is the same thing, make rhetoric his own, and do it with every article or story. English rhetoric must come alive for him. It is notorious that compilers of textbooks seldom write well; probably because they see rules rather than thoughts as their pens glide over paper. The problem for the writer who proposes to be excellent is not rules: not what is unity, but what is his governing idea; not what is coherence, but what comes next; not what is emphasis, but what part of his own idea should be driven home last and hardest.

Chapter VII

DISABILITIES AND DISEASES

RHETORIC is, after all, essentially negative; that is, in writing one uses rules and principles chiefly in analysis, in discovering what is the matter or how others have written; when writing is at its flush the place for principles is the subconsciousness. Therefore before I begin upon some practical suggestions for the writer who already knows rhetoric, yet is still clumsy in his expression, it may be useful to analyze a little further by listing in a *catalogue raisonné* some of the common diseases and disabilities of writing with special reference to their sources in faulty thinking, poverty of device, or ignorance. If the titles I choose are somewhat fanciful, that may be forgiven in a subject where the usual technical jargon has gone stale from too much use.

FLUENCY

In the very young, fluency is a virtue and usually indicates a congenital ability to write, but in maturity it is often the enemy himself. Hard writing does not necessarily make easy reading, but certainly easy writing, fluent writing, often makes hard reading for the reader who is hoping for clarity and sense. As soon as nimble words begin to skip upon the typewriter and the sound and form of sentences run ahead of the thought, the proud writer faces his greatest danger. No one really likes to toil upon an idea, to worry it, shape it, disentangle its threads, reweave them in words. Good nonsense is hard to write, but it is much easier to write little sense than sense. The quick-running fingers readily get ahead of the thought; expression outruns what is to be expressed, as a talker will often overrun his theme. The emotional pleasure in saying something that sounds well outdistances the reasoning faculty. The brain tosses whatever is ready after the flying words and drops out of the race.

A too fluent writer can do a column which will boil down to three sentences of substance. And this is why practice at writing with nothing to say becomes dangerous the moment that facility is born. The thing seems to be a paradox, for you cannot be too fluent if you are ready with your thinking, and yet any fluency is dangerous unless both consciousness and subconsciousness are ready to write. Dr. Johnson wrote *Rasselas* in a week, and would have done no better if he had taken six months. Yet there are few good novels by practiced writers, few long poems by real poets, that could not have been written through in one-quarter of the time of actual composition and in substantially their present outline; but they would not have been so good. Study the first versions of the poems of Keats as Amy Lowell printed them in her biography of the poet, and notice when his fluency misled him how carefully he corrected and strengthened his lines.

Advice here is simple enough. The writer should write as fast as possible just as long as he feels that he is saying what he wants to say, and saying it right. Never leave a crude or unfinished sentence, like an unplowed furrow, behind. Never forget the subject in the joy of writing. Never talk or write faster than you can think.

He who can write fluently will not believe a word of all this. But if he tests its conclusions by his own writing, he will find, usually, that what is written fast in a fine glow of the emotions should be rewritten in order to squeeze out irrelevancies and approach more nearly to the thought. He will find, often, that what has been written painfully, slowly, with a long search for expression, will read easily, fluently, cogently, the next morning. Cultivate fluency as you adjust for speed in an automobile, but the instant you feel fluent, put on the brakes.

The Victorians were cursed with fluency, and when their minds did not keep pace with the torrents of words which they poured out in a superabundance which we find surprising they now seem empty, like Bulwer-Lytton, tedious like Charles Kingsley, or intolerably verbose, like Ruskin or Carlyle in their worser moments.

CONGESTION

This is the opposite of fluency and comes from opposite causes. The mind moves faster than the pen.

If in moving faster it moved in a straight line, the results would not be bad. Indeed, this is what happens in good writing: the mind races through the theme or story, blazes the trail as it goes, and then returns to cut through a path of words. But in a state of congestion the mind runs in loops or circles. The thing to be said cannot be effectively said, and in trying to fit words to it the congested brain piles up qualifications, slides into digressions, checks the flow of diction, and the writing which results is of that choked and verbose style with which we are all familiar. Congestion raised above its deficiencies and made into an art is found in the later stories of Henry James, where the author's mind, like an airplane, has hovered over a single aspect of an aspect, dropping phrases upon it until the ground is covered. Congestion in its uninspired form is visible in an intolerable amount of writing where choppy sentences, broken paragraphs, and piled-up, interminable explanations wear and confuse the reader. Here is an example:

Contemporary American literature is dominated by much the same ideal of progress as American life in general, and of course progress is a natural ideal for a new country. Our writers are constantly striving to do something new, which is of course a merit in itself. They try to discover new corners of the country; they try experiments in new kinds of rhythm; indeed free verse has been written more generally by Americans than by any other nation.   There is now, however, a reaction toward old-fashioned forms.   They attempt to get at the truth about the nation by closer imitations of the way Americans act and talk.   "Main Street," a good instance of this, has however been praised abroad, and is perhaps the most famous novel in English of this decade.   But some of them are interested in a different kind of novelty, seeking new popularity rather than new truth, and these invent new thrills and unheard of romantic situations, or think up different kinds of quaintnesses for their characters, or discover unexpected tricks of plot and surprises for the endings of their stories. The "best seller" requires its own kind of novelty, and is just as difficult to progress in as the "highbrow" novel.   Americans seldom try to write as well as they can, although they work as hard as other nations over their writing.   We are in every way a strenuous race.   But perfection does not interest us so much as novelty.

And here is the same paragraph without the knots which the overloaded brain put in it:

Contemporary American literature is dominated by the ideal of progress.   Its writers are constantly striving to do something new.   They try to describe new corners of the country, they try experiments in new kinds of rhythm, they attempt to get at the truth about the nation by a closer imitation of the way Americans act and talk.   Or they invent novel thrills and unheard of romantic situations, think up different kinds of quaintness for their characters, and discover unexpected tricks of plots and surprises for the endings of their stories. They do not try to write as well as they can. Perfection does not interest them so much as novelty.

In the first paragraph the idea kept budding off to right and left and lost movement in complexity. The contrast between progress and perfection, which is the dominant idea, comes out far more clearly in the uncongested second paragraph.

Rhetorics for such faults say, "Use fewer long sentences," "Stick to the subject," "Be more concise." In revising the first paragraph such advice would be useful, and it is certainly useful for beginners practicing paragraph structure. The professional writer, however, should begin at the other end and avoid the fruits of congestion by pausing until his mind clears before he begins to write.

If his work is congested it is not because he is writing wrong, but because he is thinking wrong. His failure is due to a defect in vision. He will not, or cannot, see the whole of his thought, but only one corner at a time, and from this corner his sight glances off down some side path of thinking. If it is a scene in a story, he sticks upon a description of a room and holds up the narrative. If it is an editorial upon cosmetics, he forgets that it is the nature of vanity he is expounding while he analyzes the varieties of rouge. English sentences and English paragraphs are the most sensitive of instruments. Let the thought hesitate and they hesitate; let the thought double back and they follow. Let the thinking stop because the thinker cannot see a clear track ahead, and the sentences stop too, or exhaust their momentum in side issues and repetitions.

Congestion, of course, can result in no writing at all quite as often as in verbosity and turgidity. The writer sticks fast—the commonest of all mishaps. And often he sticks, not because he has nothing to say, but because he cannot say what is in his mind. The slow process of expression, which is a part of the difficulty of handling difficult thoughts, is not congestion at all. It is the natural and expected accompaniment of good writing when the author cannot be fluent and yet say what he wishes. I suppose that for a skilled writer at work upon an important book a thousand words a day is a good average speed. Divide a thousand words by four hours of concentrated working time (which is a day's work when the pressure is high) and one sees that slowness is a different thing from congestion. A competent writer is too full usually for quick utterance, but if his imagination keeps ahead, yet in view, of his writing, he will never become congested.

Advice, again, is easy, although a cure of congestion is more difficult to attain than a cure of fluency. He who is stuck fast in his writing should detach himself from his page and consider the whole of his purpose. He should run through his thought and consider his point. He should find the spot at which inspiration failed him and his idea ran off the track. Then he should go back to his writing and try to proceed with surer direction toward the goal he desires.

CROOKED GUIDEPOSTS

The best intelligence test for clarity, coherence, unity, and progression in writing is to be found in the transitions, whether conjunctions such as *and* and *but*, phrases such as *in any case* or *in spite of*, or clauses, sentences, and paragraphs. Every one of any education knows this; few apply it. These are the joints upon which the limbs of discourse move. It is true, of course, that by a kind of rhetorical Christian Science a good discourse may be clear and progressive with a minimum of written-down transitions. It may be so orderly in thought that transitional words are often unnecessary and sometimes impertinent. But it is not always, or often, that the reader can be trusted to do his own excepting, contrasting, adding, as he reads.

In any case, thinking by transitions is extraordinarily helpful. A lecture, once thoroughly in mind, is substantially a developing idea whose contributing thoughts are compared, added, contrasted, subtracted. Its outline in simplest terms in the memory will be "... and ... but ... nevertheless ... however ... thus ... if ... therefore ... in short," where the "..." represents in each case a step in the exposition.

And if the said lecture was muddled or digressive, thinking through in this fashion will inevitably disclose the fault. It was not, one sees, in going over the argument again, *however* at all, it was *if*. The point was not "however, we shall fight differently in the next war," but "*if* we fight differently in the next war," which means a different trend of thought. If the thinking had been straight at the beginning, the transitions, which are the guideposts of thought, would have been straight also. If the thinking is wrong, they will infallibly increase error and misunderstanding.

To recur to my first comparison, this is simply a disease of writing in which paragraphs, or episodes, or sentences, or clauses, have no proper joints between them, or no proper connectives to indicate jointing. The writing is not articulated because the thought was not articulated. It is discomposed because the thinking was not composed. The fault is in the mind; the test is the presence or absence, rightness or wrongness, of the connectives.

Direction fails also when the indicated connective, the fairly obvious *but* or *however,* is persistently left out. Young and crude and old and lazy writers are both inclined to leave out connectives where they would help to expose and make true the thinking. If a statement is *but,* make it *but*. If the idea is true *in spite of,* make it *in spite of*. If the circumstance is *indeed,* or *on the contrary,* make it so; do not leave the turn of the thought to the imagination. Many fastidious writers are afraid that they will be too obvious, afraid of pounding in their thought. Reading and study would be easier if they would be less afraid of saying just what they mean. For one writer such as Macaulay, who puts in his transitions like buttons on a coat, there are ten thousand of reputation who go unbuttoned to the discomfort of the reader.

And if the paragraphs are running in due order with a genuine relationship between each and the following, it is surprising what a difference it may make if one puts in the connectives where they are missing, inserts *nevertheless* or an equivalent sentence when it is *nevertheless* that is meant. The immediate effect will be to hold true what follows to the guide-posts of the thought. Compare these two paragraphs:

I

I detest loose thinking. The watertight compartments of Macaulay are tiresome. You can get from one to the next only by stepping across bridges of connective words. Each paragraph is crystal-clear, but each is so perfect in itself and perfectly joined to the other that you put it aside as something easily grasped, go on, and forget it. This is clear thinking and clear thinking is a virtue. Macaulay makes a fuss about his clarity!

II

I detest loose thinking. The watertight compartments of Macaulay, however, become tiresome, because you can get from one to another only by stepping across a bridge of connective words. Each paragraph is crystal-clear, but each is so perfect in itself and perfectly joined to the others that you put it aside as something easily grasped, go on, and forget it. Nevertheless this is clear thinking, and clear thinking is a virtue. If only he would be clear without making such a fuss about his clarity!

One notices that the *however,* the *nevertheless,* and the *if only* not merely raise the thought connection into visibility, they also pull the wording of the second paragraph into line with what was clearly the idea, crudely expressed, of the first.

Watch your connectives (as has been said once before) and the coherence usually will take care of itself.

LOST ZEST

There are three varieties of this disease of writing, two of which are incurable—incurable, that is, in the writing where they occur, although not necessarily in the writer.

If there is no interest whatsoever in the writing, not even the interest of doing an unpleasant job as well as it can be done, then good writing is impossible. The first paragraphs may roll sonorously but the style is sure to flatten, the expression grow feeble and empty. The only remedy is to tear up the sheets and try something else, or if they have to be written, be content to write badly.

And interest, once keen, may die en route. When the warm flush with which writing began dies away and the sentences begin to ramble, the cause is very probably not a loss of interest in the subject, it is a loss of the subject itself. The writer is no longer interested because he is no longer writing upon what interests him; his mind has skidded into a new region of thought and he is uninterested in what he finds there. Rhetorics call this a lack of unity without indicating its cause; practical writers say they have "lost the point." The fatal weak last act, which ruins many a good play, is an example. The playwright has lost his grip on his theme; his invention grows feeble, the conclusion he wished to reach he cannot reach, and so he flings together a few coincidences and pulls down the curtain.

Let us be honest. Not Shakespeare himself, as some of his work proves, could see how to end some plays effectively. It is by no means possible to carry through every idea which springs brilliantly into the mind and seems the very thing to engage the imagination. A house can always be roofed, but many an idea has no outcome in the mind of its progenitor. There seems to be no good way of completing it. More stories have been left unfinished than were ever concluded; nor has the world suffered from their loss.

This is the expected wastage in writing, and the only moral to be derived from it is to consider whether a slackening interest means no thoroughfare ahead, and if so, stop.

Curable anhedonia (which is the technical name for this difficulty) is a different matter. Like the measles it is, chiefly, a disease of youth, yet there arc always writers who in this respect seem never to grow up.

If interest slackens, if diction fails, if thoughts ramble, if expression spatters into irrelevant words, suspect first that the idea is not lost but merely blurred. Of course, if there was no aim, there is no use in coming to the clinic, but then good writing always has an aim and to stay interested must hold it. Books often dismally display the blur of wandering thoughts. Novels drop into dull chapters in the middle, or slide off into weakness at the end, solely and demonstrably because the writers have lost their zest for the writing. And they have lost their zest because they have lost, momentarily, their aim. *Vanity Fair* descends into relative dullness, and so does Booth Tarkington's *The Turmoil,* and both for the same reason. Trollope, that careless but perennially fresh gossiper, will be intolerably dull for a chapter, then see his way, recover his zest, and be interested and interesting again.

In the ordinary short-distance writing which most

of us practice, the disease is more insidious, and also more dangerous, for we do not recover but plod on dully to the end. And our anhedonia is due usually to laziness, to an unwillingness to think through at the beginning, to stop when thinking grows vague; it is due to some one of the sins against the idea discussed before, every one of which will attack interest at its root. More energy is required, unfortunately, to recognize anhedonia and go back to the switch in interest where the mind left the main line than to bump along the siding. The driver of an automobile with plenty of time on his hands will risk a doubtful turning rather than stop to ask questions, and will push on uncertainly rather than turn back. So it is in writing.

Of course, this again is just a question of good thinking; yet what one has to fight against in this particular difficulty is not so much an inability to cerebrate as a common mental habit which makes the mind go on dimly after it has lost its zest. An intolerable amount of dull, frowsy writing is the result.

The advice then is, that when the mind hesitates, grows cold, begins to labor, loses zest, you should suspect instantly a loss of direction. The climax at which you aimed, the proof that was preparing, the point of it all, is no longer so clear as it seemed at first. Go back. Wait until the mind warms again to the idea. Save time by waiting. Milton is said to have written *Paradise Regained* because his Quaker friend told him that salvation came after damnation. He was, to judge by the result, not vividly interested. Read it for a warning!

INHIBITION

If this book were designed only for creative writers I should make little reference to this difficulty, for time is sure to cure it in the born writer; but all educated men and women have to compose in writing whether or not they intend to become authors in a professional sense, and many an individual who infinitely prefers mathematics or salesmanship or executive management to the painful business of writing is forced by circumstances to become a scribbler in spite of himself. Only captains of industry, statesmen, and the great ones of the moving-picture world can have their books and articles written for them, and even they cannot usually get them written well.

That familiar blankness of brain in the young writer, that sudden constriction of words which stops a narrative in mid course, may be due to lack of interest, or sheer inability to proceed, but much oftener is a result of inhibition. The fine imagination which has warmed the opening sentences suddenly evaporates, the grasp upon the subject relaxes, words fail, and there seems to be no more to say.

I do not refer to the proneness of youth to take a large subject because it seems easy and then collapse at the second paragraph. We have grown practical in our schools and no longer encourage students to write upon "A New International Order" or "The Nature of Religion." I refer to a much more subtle disability which modern psychology helps us to understand.

In pure literature the difficulty is usually a lack of self-confidence. In explanation or argument it is often sheer fright. The atmosphere of America is still not favorable to literature. We are brought up to regard literary expression, like musical and pictorial expression, as something freakish, a gift for particular people who differ from the rest of us. We are just beginning to understand that children, with rare exceptions, have a sense for music, a sense of form, a sense for poetry and literary expression, even as they possess a sense for speech and movement. True, their potentiality may be small, but there is nothing abnormal, nothing esoteric about it, and they should take as naturally to telling stories, or to making rhythms, as to eating or playing.

In the art of literature a false teaching has impressed upon youth the rarity of literary excellence and blurred these natural capabilities. When the boy begins to write what may be called literature, whether poetry or prose, he is too much moved by the strangeness of his endeavor. He thinks not so much of what he wants to do as of what great writers have done. He is told to tremble before the mysteries of construction, metre, climax, style. His mind stiffens, his imagination chills. Doubting whether he can carry on, he finds he cannot. The mounting pressure of creation subsides. Vitality leaves him.

This is inhibition in writing with its resulting loss of energy; and that it comes from a lack of self-confidence is usually as evident as that the confidence needed is not in genius or even in talent, but merely in the power of all intelligent beings with a decent equipment to record what they wish in words that are adequate if not the ultimate best. Courage is as essential in writing as in business or the law; a willingness to push on through trial and error is as necessary as in scientific research. Without courage and a certain humble willingness to do one's best, the mind begins to falter and the writer to hesitate. If he writes on it is to mark time by empty repetition; his story stammers, his essay begins to move in circles, he sticks, or goes on badly.

The remedy for marking time is to take time by the forelock and push on. If there is creation in the mind give it a chance to work as perfectly as possible even though that is imperfectly. Things get done by the doing, and most creative work seems but a crude rendering of the imagination while it is under way. And when it is not so-called literature which is involved, but merely the pushing through of a difficult letter or article, end the fright, of which you are possibly not even aware, by forgetting what your betters might accomplish and rebending your mind upon the subject in hand with a will to do it in your own best way.

Of course there must be real ideas; but if you have ideas, a rational confidence is their best lubricant.

"WORDS, WORDS"

It has been supposed that the practical nature of an industrial civilization has made flatulency rare in modern writing. It is true that the swelling rhetoric and pompous verbosity of the early nineteenth century are now uncommon, that even a third-rate romancer is more concise than Walter Scott, and that no essayist would dare to indulge in the cataracts of words that often roared from De Quincey and Coleridge. It is no longer necessary to urge the young writer not to be florid, not to roll his phrases, not to pile up words for sound rather than sense. His own taste guards against this kind of flatulency, and his vocabulary, no longer stuffed with memories of the Latin orators, is usually incapable of Websterian effects or the wave lengths of Gibbon and Burke. Indeed, the art of oratory is suffering from a decline in real eloquence just at the moment when the radio promises to make eloquence again important.

Wordiness, however, has not been cured by an abatement in phrase-making. It has reappeared in another part of the rhetorical system, and is the more dangerous because its modern form is insidious.

Flatulency today consists in saying simply in several different ways the same thing over and over again.

The modern newspaper is a striking example. There, in order, as the textbooks say, to provide for cutting, but chiefly so that the news may reach the most sluggish intelligence, a column will consist of one paragraph rewritten with slightly different details, and an editorial be made of a few sentences molded and remolded in a paragraph of repetition. Short stories are guilty too, even though we boast of the rapidity of our narrative. Compared with the terse style of Boccaccio, our stories are overloaded with trivial, though catchy, dialogue, and upholstery of every description.

It is true that circumstances determine scope and that there is frequently a good reason for making a news column repetitious or for loading a story with realistic detail. Repetition emphasizes and description arouses the emotions and stirs the imagination. Nevertheless, there is always an accompanying loss, and no one can pile up words on his idea without danger of burying it. Henry James's narrative suffers from his infinite elaboration, yet he elaborates in order to exhaust every nuance of his situation, and his complex chapters are actually less diffuse than a story of simple action told at too great length or an argument that repeats and repeats the same elementary thought.

Flatulency is sometimes the same as fluency; it may come from an overstimulation of the faculty for words. Phrases spring ahead of the slowly clearing thought, three adjectives suggest themselves where one is suf-

ficient, and all go in and stay there. More often, it is
due to sheer laziness. It is always easier to say what
has to be said in a hundred words than in ten, and if it
can be said in ten, far less effective. Self-examination
is as useful as it is painful.

Try to condense the verbose Macaulay, the ornate
Stevenson, the skillful Sterne, the impeccable Addison.
It can be done sometimes, but it is extraordinarily
difficult to do it without losing some nicety of thought
that cannot be expressed in simpler phrase. Then take
one of your own paragraphs and rewrite it in half or
three-quarters (by count) the number of words. Take
a group of paragraphs and, first studying the essentials in the ideas expressed, rewrite the whole with as
rigorous a fifty- or sixty-per-cent space limit as a
managing editor might give you. If you cannot compress without destroying all expressiveness you are
either already concise to perfection, or unwilling, or
incapable. But if you can cut your two thousand
words to one thousand without real loss you will make
discoveries in the economy of words and see your
thought spring out as the undergrowth is cut away.
It is a lesson worth learning. What every editor
knows is that nine-tenths of the copy submitted to him
could be compressed into fifty per cent of its bulk with
profit all round.

This is from a current newspaper where an old-
fashioned floridity celebrates cotton:

From the time of its first soft, creamy, white bloom, opening its chalice to receive the dew-drops of early morn, paling in a few short hours into pink and red, to fall from the small, primitive boll, whose tiniest lobes are crucibles into which the mysterious alchemy of nature blends and fuses in the laboratory of God's Divine plan of nature; where heat and moisture and the ultra-violet or actinic rays of the sun, with other innumerable and inscrutable laws of nature, the rich oily seed and the beautiful tensile strength of its fiber, until in due process it has grown and ripened and Lo and Behold! it bursts open like a full grown rose, to start upon its intricate career of service to humanity.

And here is the delightful wordiness of Mr. Micawber, where the disability becomes a humor:

Sir—for I dare not say my dear Copperfield.

It is expedient that I should inform you that the undersigned is Crushed. Some flickering efforts to spare you the premature knowledge of his calamitous position, you may observe in him this day; but hope has sunk beneath the horizon, and the undersigned is Crushed.

The present communication is penned within the personal range (I cannot call it the society) of an individual in a state closely bordering on intoxication, employed by a broker. That individual is in legal possession of the premises, under a distress for rent. His inventory includes, not only the chattels and effects of every description belonging to the undersigned, as yearly tenant of this habitation, but also those appertaining to Mr. Thomas Traddles, lodger, a member of the Honourable Society of the Inner Temple.

If any drop of gloom were wanting in the overflowing cup, which is now "commended" (in the language of an immortal writer) to the lips of the undersigned, it would be found in the fact . . . that the living responsibilities clinging to the undersigned will, in the course of nature, be increased by the sum of one more helpless victim, whose miserable appearance may be looked for—in round numbers—at the expiration of a period not exceeding six lunar months from the present date.

After premising thus much, it would be a work of super-erogation to add that dust and ashes are for ever scattered
On
The
Head
Of
WILKINS MICAWBER.

For modern verbosity see any news story on the day after an election or a big football game.

DRY AS DUST

If the mind is arid the writing will be dry, that goes without question. Not all the good advice in the world will draw interesting copy from a mature but uninteresting mind. Yet bone-dry writing often comes from men and women who themselves are alive with personality and astir with ideas. It is well known that excellent lecturers seldom write as well as they talk; that there is a lift, a persuasiveness, a style, in their spoken words which does not get into their written prose. The converse is, of course, also true, that the best of writers are often wretched speakers; but that is not our problem.

Dryness in writing, when avoidable, is indeed just this failure to get ideas in their original warmth into written words. Any subject can be made interesting to an intelligent reader if the writer's interest is transferred to his words. Bergson, for example, is difficult, but he is never dry. No one of sense ever complained of the dryness of Darwin in spite of the voluminous detail. A dry writer is not one that you cannot understand, he is one who is dull when you understand him. Dry writing is not hard writing; it is writing that ought to be interesting and is not.

Granted personality, granted living ideas, granted a reasonable command over vocabulary and sentence structure, why should a story or an article ever be dry in this sense? There are, it seems, three reasons.

The first is the commonest. It is hard to persuade the commencing writer that he must have his project alive and complete in his imagination *while* he is writing. When he plunges into writing before his brain is ready, he breaks sooner or later like a badly trained trotting horse, and from that moment on pushes his writing ahead mechanically, completing his task, but losing his zest and failing to get flavor in his style. When he waits to write until his vision has faded, his words reflect that fading as certainly as a thermometer records temperature. The first reason for dryness is that the imagination and the pen part company; the words, instead of following a warm idea, go on along a path which may be straight but has lost its aim.⌋ The remedy is the oft-suggested cure for so many diseases of writing. See and feel your work as a whole before you begin to write. If the whole is there the parts will take care of themselves, or can be made to do so. The readiness is all. ⌈The second reason for dryness is more subtle. It is a lack in the sense for words.⌉ Words are names of ideas merely. If you use the wrong names the effect is a blur. I do not mean a lack in vocabulary. The seventeenth century pamphlet writers had remarkable vocabularies, yet their effusions are often intolerably dull because they poured out their syllables without discrimination, using words as children in a fight pick up whatever is handiest. The insufferable dullness of much sermon writing, and quite as much journalism that tries to be sprightly, is of the same origin. Every fifth term will be a stereotype, worn by use until it is shiny, or a hit-or-miss cant phrase. The sermon is strung with pompous clichés, the news story with cheap ones, but in either case the effect is of a piece on a piano played with flat notes, or a moving picture of the primitive type with blurs and flashes on the screen.

Reflect upon the essential dryness of this would-be "snappy" advertising paragraph:

Successful men who think are always the first to discover and adapt new and better things. These men make the "Old Pal" list of customers look like a "Who's Who." Broaden your field of enjoyment. Don't limit your smoking tastes to a cooped-up area. A new world will open up for *you* with this wonderful tobacco. Meet the tobacco worth knowing today.

The words here are not wrong, but in the important phrases they are seldom altogether right. Compare their stale flatness with the phrasing of this letter of Max Beerbohm's, who is never dry because his words are always just and full of life. This is his idea of an honest letter to a pushing author:

DEAR MR. EMANUEL FLOWER:

It was kind of you to think of sending me a copy of your new book. It would have been kinder still to think again and abandon that project. I am a man of gentle instincts, and do not like to tell you that "A Flight into Arcady" (of which I have skimmed a few pages, thus wasting two or three minutes of my not altogether worthless time) is trash. On the other hand, I am determined that you shall not be able to go around boasting to your friends, if you have any, that this work was not condemned, derided, and dismissed by your sincere well-wisher,

WREXFORD CRIPPS.

A sense for words can be cultivated at least as easily as the tones of the voice. Good reading, in itself, will cultivate it. Indeed, I suspect that the dryness of our more serious, and especially our scientific, writers here in America is due to the slim allowance of belles-lettres in their reading. I suspect that the shrill cleverness, so easily turned flat, of much American journalism, including many American short stories, is due to the failure of many a journalist to do any good reading at all.

"Playing the sedulous ape" to good writers, as Stevenson advised, is a dangerous game which leads toward affectation and (as in his own case) preciosity. But a tonic of excellent style, taken for half an hour a day over a long period, would be of great benefit to writers whose diction suffers from anemia to the point of dryness.

The third reason for dryness I have already mentioned. If the writer has only dry thoughts, there is no cure, at least after thirty.

BEAUTY RASH

Rashes "come out" in writing as they do upon the face. They are a symptom usually of youthful disorders and often spring from mental indigestion. It is not difficult to cure them.

Unfortunately, the writer usually thinks that his rash is beautiful; indeed, he acquires it in the attempt to be beautiful. He tries, as the Irish say, to put beauty upon his work, not realizing that the beauty must be inherent in the idea and the plan. He piles up his adjectives, fusses over his nouns, lets his rhythms swing almost into poetry, forces his note, fills out his sentences with meaningless but harmonious phrases, and determines to be literary even in his use of conjunctions.

Rough-and-ready writers never suffer from beauty rash. Journalists soon learn to escape it, for the city editor keeps drastic medicines for this disease. The chief sufferers are precisely those with whom the future of good writing must rest, the men and women (they are usually boys and girls) who are determined to write beautifully.

All English writing that rises above the most strictly utilitarian should be beautiful. But beauty is a harmony, not a plaster or a paint. The instant that sound means more than sense to the aspiring writer, the moment that he begins to think more of words than of their meanings, more of sentence rhythms than of his idea, the damage to style begins. Adjectives swell out like eruptions, fine words which are not true words pepper the page.

It is true that the sound of words is important, and often the sound will determine which of two synonyms has the right emotional content. But words cannot be emptied of meaning and used for their tone color alone. The experimenters in diction, like Gertrude Stein, who play such tricks with their English, have ended in absurdity. The beauty of diction must be a beauty proper to articulate speech. The amateur with "beauty rash," however, is seldom experimenting in

the metaphysics of language. He is at the most trying to write finely without anything very fine to say.

Like the measles, beauty rash is seldom a fatal disease, nor is it a sign of enduring weakness. Indeed,
it is often a symptom of strength—the best indication
that the sufferer may some day develop a style, whereas
the writer who never tries for beauty is doomed to
perpetual flatness.

Nevertheless, the tendency should be attacked upon
sight. Pretty writing, fine writing, swollen writing,
precious writing, cries for the blue pencil. A good
medicine is to condense, compress, reduce. Beware
of the adverb and the adjective. Think less of models
and more of ideas. Remember that writing is first and
always expression, and that a crust of ornamental
words upon a thought fully expressible by simpler
means is as incongruous as icing on a lily.

For those who write in English there is an admirable
remedy for the turgid prose, the wordiness, the false
beauty of such writing as the selection on page 90 or
the absurdity of this:

Her golden hair was like a shower of primrose petals falling, and her cheeks were finished with the artistic touches of
Aurora's rosy hand. Her eyes were like the corolla leaves of
the blue-veined violet, her nose was a posy to her face, and her
pearly teeth sparkled with nectarean dew.

The remedy is to read one hundred pages of the best
French prose which, though it may lack profundity,

has attained a simplicity, a lucidity, an economy of just words, which is beautiful without ostentation or effort. Anatole France, Voltaire, Pascal—any one of the prose writers in the true Gallic tradition will serve. Probably French poets should read English poetry; certainly every ambitious writer of English prose should learn to read French easily, the more so as in this instance he can learn without the danger of slavish imitation. The two languages medicine each other. There is a long lesson for Americans in the brief prose of Anatole France's description of the origins of our society in the penguin island:

A ce moment, le saint homme Maël, joignant les mains, poussa un grand soupir.

— Ne voyez-vous pas, mon fils, s'écria-t-il, ce furieux qui coupe avec ses dents le nez de son adversaire terrassé, et cet autre qui broie la tete d'une femme sous une pierre énorme?

— Jes les vois, répondit Bulloch. Ils créent le droit; ils fondent la propriété, ils établissent les principes de la civilisation, les bases des sociétés et les assises de l'État.

— Comment cela? demanda le vieillard Maël.

— En bornant leur champs. C'est l'origine de toute police. Vos pingouins, ô maître, accomplissent la plus auguste des fonctions. Leur œuvre sera consacrée à travers les siècles par les légistes, protégée et confirmée par les magistrats.

FAULTY BRAKES

This mechanical disorder is not quite the same as fluency, since too great fluency at the worst adulterates with words a piece essentially well ordered. "Faulty brakes" is merely a convenient term for not knowing when to stop. The brakes in this case are a function of that judgment which sees a piece to the end, and sees *the* end, before the writer writes. When they give way, the fertile mind keeps adding suggestions or incidents after the point is made, the story told. It is a garrulousness in writing which results from not knowing what is to be done and when it is done. Cutting and condensation will take care of such digressions as may have resulted en route from a weak brake control, but at the end the brakes must clamp, and if they do not, amputation is the remedy. Brakes fail in age rather than in youth, for in youth the machine is not yet speeded up and the difficulty is not to stop writing, but to write. In maturity, however (to change the figure), we begin to squeeze our ideas to the last drop, and beyond.

Sometimes the brakes come down too soon. Sometimes the manuscript is not really finished, the story lacks its conclusion, the essay its pointed ending. The two faults are aspects of the same error. To know when to stop, and when not to stop, is not difficult if your subject has been given a true beginning, an adequate middle, and a logical ending.

RICKETS

The violet ray cures rickets in children, but no painless treatment exists for the writer's disease. The bony structure of a piece of writing is its thought, its plan, the logical outline of its developing idea. If this gives way as the bones do in rickets, the whole organism suffers. Without the support of reasoned thought the fabric of writing may collapse into a jelly of words. That catastrophe occurred again and again in the height of the romantic movement, and the curious who will look through the magazines of the '30s when "sketches" and "meditations" were fashionable will find so-called literary articles that are mere congeries of words with little more stiffening than grammar and syntax could provide. Rickets is the especial disease of young girls' themes, where susceptibility so often outruns the power of observation. It is characteristic of many "feature articles" in women's magazines and women's pages, where a slender idea, borrowed from a better thinker, holds up a precarious two columns.

Men are not so often affected by this disorder, except upon the platform, where the male lecturer will often illustrate it to perfection.

Rickets in writing must be recognized before it can be cured. It is not digression, it is not fluency, it is not flatulency, although it may lead to all of these. The idea of the piece is usually clear enough, and its development easy to follow. But it will not stand the weight of words put upon it, and visibly bends until the article or story loses all firmness and much of its point.

Rickets in children comes from undernourishment, and so does rickets in writing. The author with rickets does not know enough, has not read enough, is not sufficiently experienced, to write. An editor would say of his manuscripts, "Written well, but nothing in them." If your writing suffers from rickets, what you need is medicine for your intellect and imagination. Tonic your brain and let writing wait for convalescence.

UNBALANCED, UNCONTROLLED

Glands, by their secretions, affect, when they do not control, the growth and tendencies of the human organism. Too much of one gives an excess of energy; too little of another results in smallness of stature; too much of a third overstimulates the emotions. Only when all the glands function properly does the human body meet its problems with unhampered equipment and balanced skill.

Writers suffer in somewhat the same fashion. With one, the intellect secretes too freely. If it is fiction he is writing, the technique of a story seems more important than the story itself. If it is an article, the transitions ring out like starter's guns, and the thought is rammed down your throat with nothing but pure reason to commend it. Such a writer is always trying to reduce human nature and human thinking to the likeness of the multiplication table and the precision of a machine. The great evolutionary hypotheses of Herbert Spencer suffered from this fault of over-rationality, but you need go no further than the nearest textbook on economics or sociology to find homelier examples. The intellect is an indispensable tool by which we handle reality; but reality (of which human nature is a part) is by no means comprehensible by logic. The over-intellectualized mind is forever being too clear, too logical, too emphatic, to fit the truth. All the world for him can be reduced to $2 + 2 = 4$; and if it refuses to simplify, he forces it. Every neat argument, dogmatic story, intensely reasonable essay, is open to suspicion. No writer can live in his intellect alone and be safe.

More commonly a sweet infusion of sentiment leaks momentarily into the brain and dulls or poisons those reasoning processes which after all must always function. An essay that begins cool and clear turns soft toward the end or suffuses into empty rhetoric. We are told that the "sob stuff" in the newspapers and in popular fiction is written by highly sophisticated people who are deliberately seeking a calculated effect. This is true sometimes, of course, but not of the most successful sentimental writing. The novelists who sell by the hundreds of thousands may seem to be "hard-boiled" in their lives, but actually there is something in their minds that excessively develops the softer emotions. The water of sentiment cannot rise above its source.

There cannot be too much honest sentiment in a story where sentiment belongs at all. But the glandular variety is easily recognizable by its departure from reason and truth. It is morbid, which means that there is more of it than the occasion demands. Dickens's emotions were oversensitive, and while their ready functioning gave him his power over the heart, occasionally he writes a scene so sticky with exaggerated sentiment as to annoy the reader or even disgust him. In America, any situation in which sudden wealth comes to the hero quickly, especially if youthful beauty is involved, overstimulates sentiment, and produces a type of story which is as unhealthy as it is untrue.

And yet with aspiring writers I believe that the trouble lies more often in the realm of the intellect. They secrete too much criticism (too much bad criticism especially), too many fearful memories of how others have handled such a scene as they propose to write. Not their instinctive emotions, which are honest, nor their experience, which is true, but their crudely functioning reason governs what they write. They are, as the psychologists say, inhibited from writing simply and truly, and try to compensate by a rigid and mechanical technique. Of a hundred magazine stories by current writers, ninety are more clever, neater, more skillful, than they are excellent. They are rational rather than profound. And it is notorious that the young reviewer or editorial writer will be

smart rather than sound, dogmatic rather than per-
suasive, nine times out of ten.

All this is usually curable by experience. Yet sometimes the reverse happens. The patient grows worse
as he grows older. If he began by being sentimental,
he ends maudlin. If he began by being coldly intellectual, he winds up as a mechanical writer of wooden
paragraphs intolerably dull.

Many cases are incurable. There are writers so
sentimental that they should be forbidden by statute
to write. Yet since the power to make literature is
itself an abnormality and implies abnormal development, the individual who does not suffer from too much
thinking or too much feeling will probably never make
literature at all. It is important therefore to make a
self-diagnosis, not once, but constantly, with the hope
that you may reach a balance, not by suppressing your
flow of emotion or the functions of your intellect, but
by harmonizing them. How much emotion springs
from the idea, how much from the desire to be emotional? The former makes good writing; the latter
piffle. Do you consider too curiously the means of
writing, forgetting its end, which is self-expression?
Do you develop an outline or construct a plot as if
these were problems in mathematics, thus letting the
reason strangle the thing to be reasoned about? Do
you pour out your feelings as the child cries, express-
ing nothing but your desire to express yourself? Such
questions test the relative functioning of the reason

and the emotions. The clearest mind, the best inter-
preted experience, the most sensitive perception, will
never make a good writer if either the intellect or the
emotions betray him when he begins to write.

Chapter VIII

SPECIALTIES

IT is the honest opinion of most practicing writers that if more attention were given to the principles which govern all writing, more time to good reading, and less energy expended in following courses on how to write short stories and novels, every one would benefit. A partial exception must be made for plays, where the necessity for stage adaptation leads to a special technique which in its elements can be taught, and a general exception for those niceties of structure—rhythm in poetry, order in narrative, rhetorical devices in exposition and argument—a knowledge of which will save the beginner much unnecessary error. Yet, in general, if writing comes easily, good writing will best be learned by ardent experiment, under guidance and criticism if possible.

Hence, in this chapter on specialties, I shall attempt no large discussion of particular technical problems but merely indicate as well as I can how the grasping of an idea and the expression thereof apply to the various kinds of literary composition.

THE ESSAY

The essay is, as its name implies, an assay, the trying out of a subject. In modern usage, it is the personal comment of a fruitful mind upon a theme which cannot be exhaustively developed in a brief space, but may be left richer and more suggestive. An essay, therefore, is more than a piece of logic. It makes its point, like an argument, and usually one point only, yet the sum of its writing is more than the facts it contains or conclusions it reaches. The personality of the writer carries over into the discourse and persuades to belief in proportion to the richness and force of his thinking.

An essay may be definitive, but it must always be suggestive or it is not an essay. Style, which is the result of a perfect transference of mind into words, is therefore at a premium in the essay. This is its weakness, for that bastard style which is only mannerism representing some personal idiosyncrasy is always stimulated by essay writing, and often dominates it. The merely literary essay, in which trivial things are said beautifully and the personality of the author capers upon the page, is one of the least admirable of art forms.

THE ARTICLE

The article differs from the essay only in that fact and point are more important than suggestion and the personality of the writer. It is the essay of a practical age. Yet it is an error to suppose that the subject of an article is more important than the way in which it is written. Article writing for newspapers and popular magazines is a crafty art, and a skillful writer will spend as much energy upon making his article seem simple, direct, and unliterary as Stevenson spent to accomplish the reverse.

Honest article writing is nothing but good explanation, unvarnished, unrhetorical, yet employing every device of good writing which can persuade the fact-hungry reader to read. If all ideas could be written out by arranging the facts in the case in the most attractive order, then no one need ever write essays, or poetry either. But the world is full of inexpressibles, which are as a rule more important than evident facts, and while they do not make good fodder for the literal-minded, literature must try to capture them. The article writer must be clear and orderly, he must be clever in his strategic marshaling of facts; it is not necessary for him to be subtle or suggestive. Indeed, it is dangerous.

THE SHORT STORY

Is it possible to discuss the vexed question of writing the short story in half a dozen paragraphs? I believe so, for the short story is only an attempt to tell effectively a brief story of a significant aspect of living. Just how it is told is of little importance in comparison with the significance of the life involved and the effectiveness of the telling. We have been laboring under a burden of technical terms collected for the short story—introduction, climax, conclusion, situation, plot—whereas if a short story is good without a climax, and many are, it is successful, and it makes no difference how the story is introduced if the reader is satisfied.

Indeed, the important realization for writers of the short story is that it has no complex technique of its own. There are methods of writing the short story, most of them stale, by which inventive writers have successfully given a high specific gravity to their brief narratives, or have caught in a nutshell the essence of an aspect of life. But this is *their* technique and cannot be safely standardized for general practice. The decline of the short story as an art form in the United States is largely due to a mistaken idea that a formula by which any story can be told has been discovered. It is true that a way of telling by means of which any good-enough story could be sold in a rising market has been stereotyped, but this patent will be out of date long before beginners can profit by it. As well study bicycle riding in order to learn to drive next year's automobile.

What can be learned of the short story is this: The idea must be capable of brief telling. The narrative must focus upon the heart of the story, which does not mean that every word must point toward the end. Leisure in the short story, as elsewhere, is sometimes more effective than excitement. The story when it ends must be concluded: all that needs to be told of this particular unit of life must be said or suggested. The dialogue, if there is dialogue, must be pointed and, like all the details of the story, highly relevant. It must represent actual speech with sufficient accuracy to give an illusion of real talk, and yet be condensed, elevated, refined, as real speech seldom is, in order to carry with ease and economy the idea of the story. This last difficulty must be solved in all fiction; the limitations of the short story make it rather more difficult. Beyond these requirements short-story writing involves only the problems of all narrative, where life must always be presented by a series of events, and these problems are best approached by the path to good writing in general which has been marked out in this book.

Given the imaginative power to follow and direct the stream of life, the short-story writer need only have that kind of imagination which sees short stories everywhere, and the ability to grasp and express them.

Although his vision is specialized, he writes by the laws which govern all literary art.

THE NOVEL

Is there more to say of the novel? Yes, but not in this place. Readers of this book should, most of them, be reading novels, not writing them. The impulse to write short stories or poetry should be accepted as soon as felt; the impulse to write essays and articles should wait upon knowledge and experience; the impulse to write a novel should be resisted until maturity. The novel (I do not refer to the romance which may come earlier) must employ every resource of writing discussed in these pages, for in its modern form every kind of writing, including the dramatic, the lyrical, the expository, the argumentative, and pure impressionism finds place in its narrative. Furthermore, if there is to be more than a surface skimming, or a pot-boiling of sentiment, all these must be used in the service of a sure and highly imaginative knowledge of life either in its full complexity or in its profound simplicity, or in both. First novels by writers who begin young are often promising; they are seldom excellent, and often take the edge off possible achievement. Reputations so gained are premature and too often lead to final disappointment.

The technical problem of the novel is in one sense, at least, opposite to that of the short story. Since the short story, in America particularly, has become stereotyped, it is important to forget formulated technique and, with eyes upon the subject, to search out one's own best way of writing. But the novel, technically considered, has been in a highly creative period. It has become elastic in form and fruitful in subject, and pioneers in its practice have pushed out in all directions, trying new experiments by which the appearance of reality may be vividly and truthfully presented. One need mention only Dorothy Richardson, James Joyce, Sherwood Anderson, Sinclair Lewis, Virginia Woolf, Waldo Frank. As always with experimentalists, success has been usually greater in novelty than in achievement. There has been much progress and little perfection. It will be the inheritors of innovation, with less concern for novelty and more for taste, fidelity, and achievement, who will profit by inventions which are still mobile and still applicable to new subjects and new problems. The would-be writer of novels should study technique, but, if he is young or inexperienced, he should read novels, not write them. Let him learn writing elsewhere.

DRAMA

The sense for the dramatic is inborn and cannot be taught, although of course it may be developed, chiefly, I think, by the study of literature and the seeing of plays rather than by the study of composition. Drama is essentially narrative, and the composition of drama requires fundamentally the qualities which condition any good story-telling, plus a tension greater than ordinary narrative requires. Some of these, like the sense for incident, the instinct for a situation, and the imagination which makes dramatic tension, are gifts of nature and especially of heredity. Others are dependent upon clear thinking, a grasp of the idea, training in order and development, and a knowledge of life. The conception of writing as a means to an end which has been emphasized continuously in this book is the first essential for the would-be dramatist. Granted dramatic faculty, he must learn to see the whole of his work and to grasp his idea firmly as he unrolls his dialogue. To say more of this would be to repeat what has been said again and again on earlier pages.

Note, however, that drama is explanation by means of conversation, and that therefore, even more, much more, than in fiction, the art of representing (not imitating) conversation must be studied until the dialogue expresses the characters while at the same time it moves on with the story. This must be learned, not by rules—there are no particular rules—but by observation and practice. How far the dialogue of drama (or the novel) approximates to such talk as the characters would indulge in if left to themselves, depends of course upon the aim and nature of the drama. If it is familiar and realistic, the drama is not for that reason exactly like life. No play—not even a closet drama—could get on with the rambling, inconsequential diffuseness of actual conversation. There is always a heightening and condensation of the living model. But if the play is symbolic, literary, romantic, the dialogue will depart far from the methods of ordinary speech. Even so it must give the illusion of reality, of the kind of reality which the play itself presents. Shakespeare's romantic characters speak a blank verse which has no parallel in living experience, yet they *talk,* are felt to talk, and gain reality in talking. Dialogue must express satisfactorily the characters *as they are conceived,* and furthermore advance the action of the play. The dying Hamlet's intensely poetical "The rest is silence" is more real than a feeble imitation of current slang in a prose play. Conversation, no matter how witty, which is irrelevant to the action slows down an acted play and, even when witty, bores an audience which comes to see acting, not to hear verbal cleverness.

Since there is so much technique of this kind in drama, and since even a feeble and conventional story will give pleasure upon the stage if it is really actable, youth is no reason for not writing drama. Much sheer facility has to be acquired before anything can be expressed successfully to an audience. The advice to the dramatic aspirant therefore differs from the warning to the fictitiously inclined. If you wish to write plays begin as soon as possible. There is not much danger that you will harass the public before you are ripe. And an early beginning is the more advisable because of a set of requirements for stage presentation which are not literary at all and have nothing to do with knowledge of life, or even with mere writing. The technique of the acted drama is partly dependent upon practical psychology; it is a question of the emotional reactions of the crowd and how to control them. For the rest it is stagecraft, which is a mastery of the ways and means of producing the illusion of real action in a limited area and in a limited time. For this book to enter upon such problems is folly, since in them writing is usually subordinate, or absent as a problem altogether. And furthermore, stagecraft, like biology or painting, should be studied only in a laboratory. The playwright can learn much from a master of technique, but he can learn it best while working on the stage. Let him control his writing first of all with little regard to the theater, and then apprentice to his craft.

POETRY

For other and equally good reasons I do not propose to dip deeply into the technique of poetry. The textbook treatises upon prosody, once they have explained the nature of quantity, metre, and rime, are of little value. The elaborate treatises on rhythm—especially the accentual rhythm of English, so long misunderstood—are not written, as a rule, for poets. They are analytic, not synthetic, and belong in the study, not the writing, of poetry. Furthermore, if they are profound, they are extraordinarily difficult. It is the careful and enthusiastic reading of the best poetry which develops that sense of rhythm and play of words which must be had if the technique of his poetry is to keep pace with the imagination of the writer thereof.

But practice must be constant. This book is not written for poets, who are few in number, and will find the way, if constantly pricked on by criticism, to sharpen their tools for the work of poetical expression. It is written for the poetical, who are infinitely more numerous than any but editors, and perhaps teachers, suspect.

No such practice is to be gained anywhere in composition as in the writing of verse. Those essentials of mere writing—word sense, the rhythmic swing of expression which makes writing easy and reading agreeable, conciseness, accuracy—are all inevitable in carefully written verse, even if in content and form it never rises into poetry. A curious inhibition prevents most of us from writing in poetic form. We are shameless in bad prose, but our critical sense, which education so rapidly develops, makes us reluctant to expose ourselves in the tighter-fitting garments that verse requires. If a youth is clumsy in his prose sentences, he will be ridiculous in verse, where metre and rime keep him from stringing on words until he has expressed himself. All the more reason for writing verse; and, indeed, if verse composition (which should never be called poetry) were a common practice in the schools the results would soon appear in a more cogent, simple, and expressive prose.

All the more reason for the maturing writer to attempt verse, which in his case will certainly not be bad, although it may be highly unpoetical. He may develop poetry; most probably he will merely improve (with unexpected rapidity) the precision and expressiveness of his prose.

In order to follow such a useful practice one must understand the structure of English verse, and the method by which it seeks rhythm. Elementary information is obtainable in every prosody; more still can be learned by careful reading; most of all from a poet conscious of his craftsmanship. If you wish to write good prose quickly, write verse.

CRITICISM

Criticism, like novel writing, should come late rather than early, for excellence. The power to criticize implies maturity. But criticism as a means of learning to write may and should come early. Since critical writing has its subject (though not its point) provided, must be carefully organized, and can be brief, it is the best of discipline in clear thinking and ordered writing. Furthermore, reviewing of books, which is the bread and butter of criticism, is one of the easiest means for the amateur to break into print. The reviewer, as the facile assumption goes, does not have to get something to say since he has his book to talk about, and the unfortunate practice of many newspapers, which regard reviewing as a task that any educated person can do, and do cheaply, favors the aspirant even if it debases criticism.

Reviewing differs from criticism only in this, that since the review is usually of a new book, news of the book is as important as a critical estimate. The new book must be defined, described, explained; otherwise the general principles of criticism apply to reviewing, as the principles of good writing apply to both.

There is nothing in the application of these principles of good writing which differs from what has been said of writing in general, except that the emphasis changes. A criticism *must* have point, and preferably one point. It is an attempt to estimate, which means in a large sense an attempt to classify. Mere praise or mere condemnation does not classify. A piling up of vague descriptive phrases gets nowhere in criticism. An analysis, however acute, which leads to no conclusive opinion may be useful but is not criticism.

A good review answers the question: "Is the book good or bad or both, and why?" with the emphasis on the *why*. To paraphrase Goethe, the reviewer should ask, "What has the writer wished to do? Has he done

it? Was it worth doing?" Criticism therefore must
be cogent, directed, conclusive, or questions will never
get their answers. This does not mean that enthusiastic, emotional appreciation, with no analysis
behind it, is worthless. Appreciation which kindles
the spark of interest in the reader is invaluable, but it
is twice as effective when it is critical, when it reaches
a valid conclusion.

Compare the following passage, which is mere
enthusiasm:

Never have I sat by a roaring fire and read a romance
which so completely seized my imagination and lifted me into
the land of faëry. Mr. Smith's new novel is vivid, true, and
beautiful. It is the best fruit of his genius.

with this passage from Swinburne, which flames with
interest even though there is little criticism in it:

Had *The Changeling* not been preserved, we should not have
known Middleton: as it is, we are more than justified in
asserting that a critic who denies him a high place among
the poets of England must be not merely ignorant of the
qualities which involve a right or confer a claim to this position, but incapable of curing his ignorance by any process
of study. The rough and rapid work which absorbed too much
of this poet's time and toil seems almost incongruous with
the impression made by the noble and thoughtful face, so
full of gentle dignity and earnest composure, in which we
recognize the graver and loftier genius of a man worthy to

hold his own beside all but the greatest of his age. And that age was the age of Shakespeare.

and this from Poe, which is criticism proceeding with the emotions at work but the intellect in control:

"The Hollow of the Three Hills" [Hawthorne's] we would quote in full had we space;—not as evincing higher talent than any of the other pieces, but as affording an excellent example of the author's peculiar ability. The subject is commonplace. A witch subjects the Distant and the Past to the view of a mourner. It has been the fashion to describe, in such cases, a mirror in which the images of the absent appear; or a cloud of smoke is made to arise, and thence the figures are gradually unfolded. Mr. Hawthorne has wonderfully heightened his effect by making the ear, in place of the eye, the medium by which the fantasy is conveyed. The head of the mourner is enveloped in the cloak of the witch, and within its magic folds there arise sounds which have an all-sufficient intelligence. Throughout this article also, the artist is conspicuous—not more in positive than in negative merits. Not only is all done that should be done, but (what perhaps is an end with more difficulty attained) there is nothing done that should not be. Every word *tells*, and there is not a word which does *not* tell.

Criticism is not a science. Flashes of intuition frequently come nearer the truth than elaborate rational processes, a loving description may convey more than the coolest logic. But criticism should use science, in so far as science in literature means knowledge, accuracy, investigation, and desire for the truth.

The hard intellectual outline which, as I have tried to make clear before, supports all good writing, even the most imaginative, is most evident in criticism. Insight, sympathy, interpretative imagination, the qualities which make a great critic, can scarcely be taught, although, like the sense for the dramatic, they may be cultivated by training, especially by the self-training of the widely read. But the analysis of the processes of composition, the study of its purpose and its method in order to point out the nature and reason of failure or success, is teachable and is education in a very real sense. Furthermore, the writing which results is about as good a training as any writer can desire. Every one should review books—though few should be allowed to print their reviews. Writers will profit, even though they do not become Coleridges, Arnolds, and Poes.

Indeed, what is called the exploratory method in the education of youth might well be adapted to the teaching of writing. No potential writer should feel that he has completed his education until he has flung himself and his ideas and his abilities into attempts at essay, article, story, play, poem, and criticism.

CHAPTER IX

HINTS FOR PRACTICE

EVERY one who writes of writing says more of what not to do than of what ought to be done. Physicians are like that also; they always speak more often of disease than of health. And this is not unnatural, for what ought to be done is simple in so far as it can be explained at all, whereas the don'ts of detailed error are numerous and complex. I shall append here only a few general suggestions which are better stated positively than negatively. Like everything else in this book, after the first chapters, they repeat with variation what has been said before.

SEEING IT WHOLE

The writers' prime necessity might almost be summarized by urging him to see his task, first, last, and always, as a whole. This is a mental habit that every one with adequate mentality can acquire. It is a habit that springs, not so much from knowing just what you are going to write as where you are going, and consists in looking backward and forward constantly along the road. There should be at every moment of writing a hovering consciousness of the whole idea, the whole plot, the whole scene, which in no way interferes with the free fertility of thought, but does keep it growing in the right direction. Note, for example, Emerson's disjointed paragraphs which make his essays, for all the excellence of content, such difficult reading. Emerson, when he thought, saw his subject whole; but he did not always see it whole as he wrote. As he wrote, he went back to his notebooks for materials, and made his essays from paragraphs written under the dominance of a single idea but with little direct reference to each other. Shallower men, like Stevenson or Hazlitt, are better reading than Emerson for this reason.

With lesser minds this seeing by parts only is fatal, for there is no dominating idea toward which all sense radiates. Bad writing is bad again and again because of it. Keep one eye upon the field while you plow each single furrow.

BEGINNING AND ENDING

Begin at the beginning and end when you are done. How simple is this platitude, upon which I have already rung changes, and yet how difficult to put into practice! What is the common beginning? Oftentimes a wearisome introduction. What is the common end? Often a needless repetition or absurd anticlimax. For such ills I have already suggested medicine, yet, as a result of the stereotyped methods of teaching writing, the maturing author may need more specific advice. The beginning is *not* the beginning of the subject. You begin upon your subject when the reader has been made ready, and that may mean coaxing explanation or a warming of his mind. And you end, not when you are through with your subject, but through with *him;* when he knows, and is satisfied.

Ending and beginning are therefore questions of tact as much as logic; although logic must show where an ending or a beginning is possible before tact can come into play. Rhetorics which merely command an Introduction and a Conclusion for every discourse are standardizing this advice, and rendering it valueless; for there is no such thing as a good Introduction, there are as many possible Introductions as there are subjects to write of, and each must be composed in the light of governing circumstance. "How shall I begin? How end?" are worthy questions, to which the answers come not in terms like "Preface" and "Summary" but in concrete sentences and paragraphs composed for the particular occasions.

GOOD MANNERS

Imagination about writing is almost as important as imagination in writing. A great deal depends in a story or an essay or a letter upon how the subject is approached, picked up, conceived. The preliminary maneuvers are no more and no less important than politeness, courtesy, manners in life. Some writers burst in upon their theme with garish violence and leave it with an exclamation, others say invariably the one word which is too much. In manuals of composition too little consideration is accorded to that sense of audience which often determines success by its presence and failure by its lack. Not even a diary is written exclusively for oneself. And it is unquestionable that the writer who modestly but invariably feels the presence of an outer mind for which he writes acquires a tact and an adroitness which are invaluable. Bad-mannered writers, like Carlyle or H. L. Mencken, who bludgeon their readers, self-centered writers, like Henry James, who are sometimes indifferent to them, write under restrictions which only excellence can overcome.

Manners in writing help to determine, among other things, the effectiveness of what is said. The modernist who shocks gentle readers by calling every spade a dirty spade cannot complain if his realism is more noticeable than his art. Lacking imagination to guess the effect of his writing upon personalities that differ in taste from his own, he is disgusted when his unimportant indecencies make more impression than the ideas upon which they are merely a fringe. Such a writer does not lack morality—he may be more essentially moral than many a mealy-mouthed sentimentalist—but he does lack good manners, which is to say, good taste. Good manners of course in themselves never make good writing, but writing has to be very good in order to succeed without them. Here is an ill-mannered piece from Walt Whitman trying to bastinado his audience into attention:

This now is too lamentable a face for a man,
Some abject louse, asking leave to be, cringing for it,
Some milk-nosed maggot blessing what let it wing to its hole.
This face is a dog's snout sniffing for garbage,
Snakes nest in that mouth, I hear the sibilant threat . . .
This is a face of bitter herbs, this is an emetic, they need no label,
And more of the drug-shelf, laudanum, caoutchouc, or hog's lard.

No directions are needed here that are not applicable to good living in civilized human society. Suavity, grace, good nature, these are all valuable in their place, but good manners have a broader scope. Every writer has his own manners; every subject, harsh, angry, cutting, or amiable, has its own good- or bad-mannered way of expression.

THE SENTIMENTAL

Sentimentality is the curse of writing in America. In advertisements and circulars it is manifest in a familiarity which soon disgusts even the naïve reader.

We all know the letter from an utter stranger trying to sell something which begins, "I'm going to talk to you as one red-blooded man to another," or the advertisement of a tobacco trust headed, "Dear old Pal." The personal note in modern advertising is so obviously insincere that one must conclude that it succeeds because it is advertising, not because it is personal.

In fiction, sentimentality is more subtle, consisting with us in a plot which forces every situation to yield wealth, beauty, and easy happiness to the hero. Even the most "hard-boiled" short stories in popular magazines are sentimental when looked at squarely. They pretend to be realism but actually are conscious and purposeful romance passed off upon the gullible like spurious coin. Real romance, which expands life instead of falsifying it, is a very different affair.

In article writing the sentimental has run away with us. The "feature writer" develops a fatal gift for suffusing his writing with an unnatural and (as I have said before) an unhealthy interest. I mean that he is far more interested in interesting the reader than in his own subject. He takes the sensational aspect of some honest man's idea and plays up its pathos or excitement with a ruthless disregard of essential values. Let a historian write of the ideal of chastity in the Middle Ages and some clever charlatan will make out of his book an article on sex and wearing apparel. Even the total eclipse of 1925 was sentimentalized by writers who saw a chance to exploit mystery or terror—fortunately without success.

In a country of widespread half-education such sentimentalism is sure to be rife. The fully educated detest it; the uneducated are too close to reality to be touched by its glamour. But the vast bourgeoisie of America respond to such crude emotionalizing and writing of this kind has had vast financial rewards.

Yet it is a dangerous game to play. The writer who learns it (and it can readily be learned) in order to serve his own financial ends concludes by losing his sense of values. If he is a born sentimentalist, like Zane Grey, Harold Bell Wright, or Dr. Frank Crane, he can be assured of that permanent success which always comes to perfection on any plane. But a second-rate insincere sentimentalist is condemned to hack work for life. Follow your own "dharma," as the Hindus say: there is no stable success except through self-realization.

DETACHMENT

The writer must be able to sink in his subject; he must be equally able to rise and stand above and beyond it. A sense of humor is worth gold to any writer, for it keeps his soul detached from his problem; an artist's conscience is equally serviceable. Belief that writing is a profession and must be done professionally is a great help, for the concern to say it right which follows gives that perspective of your own work which is detachment. It is a certain detachment from the job as such which makes the sense of audience easy to acquire.

Maturity in fine natures brings detachment with it; the mind, as it becomes more and more conscious of its powers, keeps its entity distinct from the thoughts that it is shaping. Only a bungler cuts himself with his own tools. Work into your subject and then work out again to see what you have. Handle your theme as a painter handles his canvas. His mind is on his lines and colors, and yet he himself is there at arm's length, studying the whole he is creating.

Chapter X

WHO SHOULD AND WHO SHOULD NOT WRITE: SIMPLE TESTS IN THE CHOICE OF A VOCATION

THE reader of this book who is involved only in the daily business of easy thinking and accurate expression may skip this chapter. It does not concern him. But if he is what is currently named a literary aspirant, if he believes secretly or openly that a career of authorship may be possible for him, then it is vital. And if he expects to write what others may wish to read,. even though his literary ambitions are light, then it concerns him.

There are many men and women who have never dared to create in words who should emphatically try to do so, if only for self-expression. There are probably many more now pumping honest energy into writing for the public who would be much better employed elsewhere and otherwise. Writing for public expression when there is no genuine talent is likely to result only in discouragement for the writer and distress for unfortunate readers.

Is there any way in which the born writer may be diagnosed before he is successful? No sure way; yet there are useful tests.

The first is desire. Will to write is quite different from the love of good writing. Writing is hard work always, except in rare moments of easy and dangerous inspiration. It is always hard to begin writing, and usually hard to keep at it. Therefore one may dislike intensely the labor of composition and yet desire to write. But if you have passed through adolescence into youth without adventuring into prose or verse except under compulsion, you may be reasonably sure that the faculty was never born in you. Competence in expression is possible for you of course, but authorship is never your profession.

The second test is determination. If, desiring to write, you cannot force yourself to the drudgery of writing, you may be a "mute, inglorious Milton," but you certainly will never be an author.

The third test is words. The born writer is interested in words precisely as the born athlete is interested in scores or records. He collects them without meaning to do so, he experiments with them unconsciously, his vocabulary, at any given age, is richer than other men's. He may be slangy or inaccurate or ignorant, yet he has more words in proportion to his experience than the normal individual, and those words mean more to him. They are not merely counters of expression; they have colors, shades; pictures go with them; one is more valuable than another; they are nuts which his curiosity is always cracking to find the kernel of essential meaning. The born writer hears language as the musician hears tones. Style is impossible without such a native sense for words.

The fourth test is inventiveness. This is a trickier gauge than the others for there are excellent writers—Macaulay and Roosevelt are instances—who write well upon themes provided for them by history yet show little power to invent. The writer to whom an idea for a story or poem never comes may yet prove to be an essayist or journalist of great power and versatility. Yet dramatists, poets, novelists, short-story writers, must be inventive. The future story-teller will show his inventiveness long before he can write effectively. Plots (not necessarily good plots) will come to him readily. Situations, often crude and imitative at first, will be in his mind constantly. If you say, "Tell me a story," he may not be able to do it, but something in his imagination will respond which would be a story if he could shape it and get it out. The most inventive writers are not necessarily the best, for a novelist with a slender narrative sense, like Thomas Hardy, will force out great novels in his maturity by sheer obsession with life. Nevertheless, inventiveness is a prime asset, and if, as boy or girl, you do not invent easily and frequently, the road to authorship of the creative kind is sure to be rocky. Poets, especially, have almost without exception begun to invent poetical ideas in early youth.

The fifth test, which cannot be self-imposed, is probably the surest of all. Successful expression is never merely a question of the proper words. It requires, for reasons implicit in the movement of life itself, a rhythm to make it effective. The explanation is difficult, and carries far into metaphysics, the fact is evident.

Compare these two sentences:

Beautifully vague though the English language is, with its meanings merging into one another as softly as the facts of landscape in the moist English climate, and much addicted though we always have been to ways of compromise, and averse from sharp, hard, logical outline, we do not call a host a guest, nor a guest a host.

The English language is beautifully vague and its meanings merge into one another like the facts of the soft, moist English climate, and we have been always addicted to compromise and do not like sharp, hard, logical outlines, yet we do not call a host a guest, nor a guest a host.

The words are substantially the same, but the first sentence moves upon a rhythm, the second does not. One is expressive, the other expresses but not with effectiveness.

The potential author has some subtle power to bend the rhythm of speech to the rhythm of his emotions. Phrases come to him linked with other phrases; one order of words seems right, another of the same words does not satisfy. His early writing may be crude and inaccurate, yet there is movement in it. It has a pattern.

I doubt whether, in his formative stages, the writer himself can ever know whether he possesses this instinct for rhythm; it is too much a part of his subconsciousness, too much, indeed, a part of himself. Yet others can tell him. A wise critic can guess for him in early youth, and be reasonably sure by college age. He cannot be sure, of course, of real ability and the promise of genuine achievement, but he can tell whether the power is there. Of two freshman themes, one may be correct to the last comma and sentence construction, the other misspelled, awkward in spots, perhaps diffuse and obscure. Yet the first in its plod of sentences gives out not one ray of hope for literary success. Its writer will always be clear and exact; he can never be really expressive. The other, in spite of its crudities, moves; there is a stumbling life in its rhythms. Its author may always be confused, inaccurate, uneven, and therefore inexpressive, yet it is possible for him to write finely.

The final test, if one has the patience to wait for it, is success. Wise critics are rare; faculties sometimes develop late. If the desire to write is impelling, deficiencies in the other categories need not discourage finally until there is proof of failure. Failure itself is an ambiguous word. Failure to publish is not a final test, at least in youth. Literary genius that never gets published is so rare as to be almost nonexistent, but writers who are not geniuses, and many who are, must find their audiences, and this takes time. Failure to be widely popular is no certain test. If you have the will to authorship, keep on trying and let those who will not read you go hang. If you were not born to create, a moment will come when human nature steps in and gently extinguishes the desire to write.

Chapter XI

EQUIPPED

I RETURN at the end of this book to the theme of its beginning. Mere writing can be learned and taught, and its essentials—grasp and development of an idea, lucidity, scope, point—are essentials for literature as well as for the most utilitarian production. Equipment for authorship involves much that is only associated with composition. It implies knowledge, imagination, inventiveness, power over rhythm and over words, and, most of all, ideas worth bothering over. But golden boys and girls who are to become famous need the same technique of plain expression as dictators of business letters and makers of reports. They must make bread before they can butter it, although that analogy is inexact since in authorship the butter must be part of the bread. Let us say that they must bake bread before they can make cake.

And it is well known by every editor and critic that many a writer of reputation has only reputation and not fame because, while possessing invention, imagination, and facility, he has never learned thoroughly how to write. This is especially true in America where success comes easily and a novelist or story-

writer is often content with his craftsmanship as soon
as he begins to publish readily, and so stops short of
possible achievement.

I have tried to indicate what the creative writer
needs, and to insist upon what every writer must have,
whether his work passes into high imagination or stays
on the plane of obvious fact and its explanation. The
idea must be grasped, must grow in the mind, must
be fastened to paper by its essential topics and transitions, must be surveyed as a whole until it is wholly
yours. Then, with complete freedom to twist or turn
or alter as the active mind suggests, writing begins,
and composition proceeds in words. If, writing this
way, your vocabulary comes to life, your grip upon
phrases tightens, your sense for rhythm grows, your
effort translates itself more and more exactly into
results, why, then you will write well. That is a
power which in a civilization conducted by speech,
letter, and print all men desire. And if the Lord intended you to be an author, such writing will make
you a good one.

INDEX

139